International Transactions in Remittances

Guide for Compilers and Users

Eurostat

International Monetary Fund

Organisation for Economic Co-operation and Development

World Bank

INTERNATIONAL MONETARY FUND

2009

Production: IMF Multimedia Services Division
Typesetting: Alicia Etchebarne-Bourdin

Cataloging-in-Publication Data

International transactions in remittances: guide for compilers and users. [Washington, D.C.]: International Monetary Fund, 2009.

p.; cm.

ISBN 978-1-58906-825-4
"International Monetary Fund; World Bank; Organisation for Economic Co-operation and Development; Eurostat."
Includes bibliographical references and index.

1. Emigrant remittances—Statistics—Handbooks, manuals, etc.

1. Title. II. International Monetary Fund.
HG3891 .I58 2009

Please send orders to:
International Monetary Fund, Publication Services
700 19th Street, N.W., Washington, D.C. 20431, U.S.A.
Tel.: (202) 623-7430 Fax: (202) 623-7201
E-mail: publications@imf.org
Internet: www.imfbookstore.org

Table of Contents

Tables

Figures

Boxes

Foreword

We are pleased to introduce the first-ever manual providing detailed guidance on the compilation of remittances, *International Transactions in Remittances: Guide for Compilers and Users* (*RCG*). Data on remittances are important for policymaking, analysis, and research purposes. Using the detailed guidance provided by the *RCG*, economies will be able to substantially improve the quality of these data.

The *RCG* was authored by members of the Luxembourg Group on Remittances, a working group that was composed of representatives of the International Monetary Fund, the Organization for Economic Co-operation and Development, the Statistical Office of the European Communities, the World Bank, and representatives from national statistical offices and central banks from economies throughout the world. The IMF Committee on Balance of Payments Statistics also made valuable contributions. We would like to thank all of the national and international experts involved for their invaluable assistance.

Remittance transactions have grown in importance over the past decade. In a number of developing economies, receipts of remittances have become an important and stable source of funds that exceeds receipts from exports of goods and services or from financial inflows on foreign direct investment.

But the quality of statistical remittance data is not high. Remittances are a challenge to measure because of their nature. They are heterogeneous with numerous small transactions conducted by individuals through a wide variety of channels.

The economic significance of remittances, and concern for the reliability and consistency of the estimates of remittances, prompted the G-8 Heads of State to call for improvements in the quality of statistical data on remittances.

The sixth edition of the *Balance of Payments and International Investment Position Manual* (*BPM6*) addressed the definitional issues associated with international labor mobility, including remittances. The *RCG* addresses the need for practical compilation guidance to improve the quality of estimates. The *RCG* is the first compilation guide based on the concepts set out in *BPM6*.

We recommend the *RCG* to compilers and users. We urge economies to consider the practical compilation guidance provided in the *RCG* to improve the quality of their data on remittances.

Adelheid Burgi-Schmelz
Director
Statistics Department
International Monetary Fund

Enrico Giovannini
Chief Statistician and Director
Statistics Directorate
Organization for Economic Co-operation and Development

Walter Radermacher
Director General
Statistical Office of the European Communities

Shaida Badiee
Director
Development Data Group
Development Economics Vice Presidency
World Bank

Acknowledgments

In response to requests from policymakers, compilers, and other data users, the International Monetary Fund (IMF) and the World Bank invited experts in remittances statistics from selected economies and international organizations to identify a set of best practices, and to prepare a compilation guide, for remittances statistics. The first meeting of the group was held in Luxembourg (and thus named the "Luxembourg Group") in June 2006. It identified data sources and compilation methods, and it drafted and reviewed the *International Transactions in Remittances: Guide for Compilers and Users* (also called *Remittances Compilation Guide*, or *RCG*), during 2006–08. The IMF coordinated the preparation and edited the text of the *RCG.*

The members of the Luxembourg Group were Beth Alarilla (Bangko Sentral ng Pilipinas), Javier Alvarez (Bank of Spain), Kenneth Coates (Centre for Latin American Monetary Studies—CEMLA), Neil Fantom (World Bank; Mr. Fantom was the World Bank coordinator with the IMF on this project), Carla Ines Ferreira (Bank of Portugal), Mushtaq Hussain (Eurostat), Toshie Kori (Bank of Japan), Fernando Lemos (Banco Central do Brasil), Michael Mann (Bureau of Economic Analysis, United States), Tom Orford (Office of National Statistics, United Kingdom), Giuseppe Ortolani (Banca d'Italia), Tamara Razin (IMF, formerly of the National Bank of Moldova), Jens Reinke (IMF), Evis Rucaj (Bank of Albania), Claude Saadeh (Central Bank of Lebanon), Bhupal Singh (Reserve Bank of India), Jens Walter (Deutsche Bundesbank), and Bettina Wistrom (Organization for Economic Cooperation and Development). Ms. Razin and Mr. Reinke were the IMF coordinators on the project. All members made important contributions to the *RCG*, which are gratefully acknowledged. The diversity of experience of this group helped to ensure that a wide variety of remittance flows, data sources, and compilation practices were considered, and that the resulting *RCG* has the widest possible appeal.

The Secretariat for the Luxembourg Group consisted of the IMF, World Bank, and Eurostat. The three meetings of the Luxembourg Group were hosted by Eurostat (June 2006), Deutsche Bundesbank (December 2006), and Banco Central do Brasil (June 2007). The United Nations Statistics Division led the work that resulted in the adoption of improved definitions for major remittance aggregates.

The *RCG* also benefited from the expert advice of the members of the IMF Committee on Balance of Payments Statistics.

Within the IMF, the *RCG* was prepared under direction of the chiefs of the Balance of Payments Division of the IMF's Statistics Department, Neil Patterson (2006) and Ralph Kozlow (2007 forward). In addition, Emmanuel Kumah, Deputy Chief, Tamara Razin, Senior Economist, and Pontsho Mochipisi, Special Appointee, contributed to the project. Esther George and Marlene Pollard, also of the Balance of Payments Division, prepared the drafts of the *RCG* for publication.

The contributions of the above experts and staff are gratefully acknowledged. Their experience and expertise were essential to the success of the project.

List of Abbreviations

ATM	automated teller machine
BEA	United States Bureau of Economic Analysis
BIS	Bank for International Settlements
BNB	Bulgarian National Bank
BoA	Bank of Albania
BOPSY	*Balance of Payments Statistics Yearbook*
BPM5	*Balance of Payments Manual*, fifth edition (1993)
BPM6	*Balance of Payments and International Investment Position Manual*, sixth edition (2008)
CEMLA	Centre for Latin American Monetary Studies
CPSS	Committee on Payment and Settlement Systems
DQAF	Data Quality Assessment Framework
EU	European Union
FATF	Financial Action Task Force
FinCEN	Financial Crimes Enforcement Network
FTS	funds transfer system
GATS	General Agreement on Trade in Services
GDDS	General Data Dissemination System
GDP	gross domestic product
GEP	*Global Economic Prospects*
IADB	Inter-American Development Bank
IFS	*International Financial Statistics*
IHSN	International Household Survey Network
IMF	International Monetary Fund
INSTAT	Albanian Institute of Statistics
IRnet	International Remittance Network
ITRS	international transactions reporting system
LFS	Labor Force Survey
LSMS	Living Standard Measurement Study
MTO	money transfer operator
NPISH	nonprofit institution serving households
OCC	Office of the Controller of the Currency (United States)
OECD	Organization for Economic Cooperation and Development
OFWs	overseas Filipino workers
RCG	*International Transactions in Remittances: Guide for Compilers and Users*
SIM	Subscriber Identity Module
SNA	System of National Accounts
SOF	Survey of Overseas Filipinos
SWIFT	Society for Worldwide Interbank Financial Telecommunication
UNICEF	United Nations Children's Fund

CHAPTER

I Background and Purpose of the *International Transactions in Remittances: Guide for Compilers and Users*

A. Background

1.1. Remittance flows have increased rapidly in recent years. From 2001 to 2007, remittance receipts reported in the IMF's *Balance of Payments Statistics Yearbook* (measured as global receipts of "workers' remittances" and "compensation of employees") more than doubled to US$336 billion (Table 1.1). This sharp increase is linked to rising migration and labor mobility, more liberal and competitive financial intermediaries, and improved data recording. For some countries, receipts from remittances exceed receipts from the export of goods and services and from financial inflows on foreign direct investment.

1.2. Remittances essentially represent household income from foreign economies arising mainly from the temporary or permanent movement of people to those economies. However, formal definitions are slightly broader than this because they are based on balance of payments definitions that are not based on the concepts of migration, employment, or family relationships. Remittances include funds that flow through formal channels, such as electronic wire, or through informal channels, such as cash carried across borders in pockets. They may consist almost entirely of funds sent by individuals who have migrated to a new economy and become residents there, and of net compensation of border, seasonal, or other short-term workers who are employed in an economy in which they are not residents.

1.3. Many governments now consider remittances to be of high policy interest and wish to analyze their impact on economic development and security. The Group of Eight (G-8) Heads of State have been promoting improvements in the availability of statistical data on remittances. At their 2004 meeting at Sea Island, Georgia (United States), the G-8 Heads of State identified remittances as an important factor in defining their relationships with developing countries. Their concerns were brought together at an international meeting in January 2005, hosted by the World Bank and the IMF, where data compilers and data users from around the world sought to set an agenda for improving remittances data. Subsequent G-8 meetings, including the summit in Hokkaido Toyako, Japan, in July 2008, reaffirmed data users' interest in improving data. Also, international institutions, including the World Bank, the Bank for International Settlements, and regional development banks, have programs devoted to analyzing remittances. These institutions and others consider remittances to be an important anti-poverty tool and are striving to lower the costs and other barriers to sending remittances, and to facilitate the transfer of remittances via formal channels through improved regulatory and institutional arrangements.

1.4. Despite the high level of interest in remittances, evidence suggests that data on remittances are less reliable than are data on many other items in the balance of payments accounts. At a global level, remittance receipts consistently exceed remittance payments, and the gap has been growing in recent years, indicating growing inconsistencies in the coverage and compilation of remittances data. Some data users lack confidence in the estimates of remittances. Furthermore, remittance-related items in the balance of payments framework up through the fifth edition of the IMF's *Balance of Payments Manual* (*BPM5*) were defined in ways that made identification and analysis of remittances difficult for some data users.

1.5. Emerging from the January 2005 World Bank/IMF meeting was a consensus that a process for improving data on remittances required two steps: first, simplifying, clarifying, and expanding the definitions of remittance-related items to meet the needs of data users; second, developing practical compi-

Table 1.1. Compensation of Employees and Workers' Remittances, 2001 to 2007
(In millions of U.S. dollars)

	2001	2002	2003	2004	2005	2006	2007
Compensation of employees							
Credit	43,517	49,475	60,096	70,714	76,460	82,602	98,934
Debit	51,030	57,312	67,926	76,463	84,883	95,144	113,975
Global discrepancy	7,513	7,837	7,830	5,749	8,423	12,542	15,041
Workers' remittances							
Credit	81,168	93,410	112,693	126,007	153,009	180,715	237,396
Debit	67,612	77,829	81,465	91,780	99,853	117,259	135,748
Global discrepancy	–13,557	–15,582	–31,228	–34,228	–53,156	–63,457	–101,648
Sum of compensation of employees and workers' remittances							
Credit	124,686	142,885	172,789	196,721	229,469	263,318	336,330
Debit	118,642	135,141	149,391	168,242	184,736	212,403	249,722
Global discrepancy	–6,043	–7,745	–23,398	–28,479	–44,733	–50,915	–86,608

Source: IMF, *Balance of Payments Statistics Yearbook 2008*, Part 2.

Note: This table uses *Balance of Payments Manual* (fifth edition) definitions. In particular, "workers' remittances" is defined as current transfers from employment income by migrants who are employed in new economies and considered residents there. In the list of standard components for the balance of payments accounts, "workers' remittances" has been replaced in the sixth edition by "personal transfers" (however, the latter term is defined more broadly).

lation guidance to support compilers. The meeting recognized that the improvements in remittances concepts could be better achieved using the balance of payments framework and recommended the creation of a "city group" of experienced compilers to prepare a set of best practices for remittances statistics in the form of a compilation guide.

1.6. The sixth edition of the *Balance of Payments and International Investment Position Manual* (*BPM6*) completed the review and improvement of the conceptual framework of remittances. The new concepts are summarized in Chapter 3 of *International Transactions in Remittances: Guide for Compilers and Users* (*RCG*). The *RCG* seeks to support data compilers in their effort to provide accurate, complete, and timely data on remittances consistent with the improved concepts and definitions.

B. Purpose of the *RCG*

1.7. The purpose of the *RCG* is to promote lasting improvements in remittances data. It seeks to accomplish this purpose by summarizing the definitions and concepts related to remittances in the balance of payments framework and by providing practical compilation guidance.

1.8. The biggest obstacle to improving data on remittances is the nature of the flows, often involving small transactions by private individuals using a variety of transaction channels, many of which are informal or personal. The small size of individual transactions means that they often go undetected by typical data source systems, although the aggregate level of transactions may be substantial. As a result, the *RCG* focuses on the problems of and solutions to obtaining better source data on remittance transactions, but it also summarizes compilation and data dissemination issues. The *RCG* draws on the Data Quality Assessment Framework (DQAF) for balance of payments statistics to highlight good practices in data compilation and dissemination.

1.9. Although the *RCG* is primarily aimed at those whose task is to compile and disseminate data on remittances, it may also be useful for other users who wish to understand the limitations of the data. Remittances are complex to measure, and the compilation practices may not be perfect. An understanding of the data limitations will promote more informed and appropriate uses of remittances data.

1.10. The *RCG* was written for professional use, but care was taken to make it accessible to nonspecialists. The authors hope that it will be easy to understand and to use. The *RCG* is not prescriptive. Instead, it discusses alternative approaches and data sources for measuring remittances and provides guidance on the development of a statistical program for improving remittances data.

It draws on recent experiences and best international practices. The *RCG* acknowledges that country circumstances differ vastly and that compilers need to develop data compilation strategies based on the needs, constraints, and capabilities of their own countries. Experts in remittances from several countries and organizations contributed to the *RCG*. The diversity of experience of these authors helped to ensure that a wide variety of remittance flows, data sources, and compilation practices were considered, and that the resulting *RCG* has the widest possible appeal.[1]

C. Organization of the *RCG*

1.11. Following this introduction, Chapter 2 discusses the institutional and regulatory context of remittances, including demographic issues and transaction channels. It also introduces a structured approach to improving remittances data. Chapter 3 discusses relevant concepts and definitions. Chapter 4 includes several sections that discuss different approaches to obtaining data on remittances. Chapter 5 reviews good compilation practices with a focus on remittances, and Chapter 6 concludes with a look at dissemination options.

D. Terminology Used in the *RCG*

1.12. In the balance of payments framework, there is no single item or account known as "remittances." In the *RCG*, the word *remittances* will be used to refer to the remittance-related items in the balance of payments framework. These transactions are often related to migrants and short-term workers and frequently involve households on both the sending and receiving ends. As set out in Chapter 3 of the *RCG*, it will always refer to the appropriate balance of payments terminology in a technical context. In the *RCG*, remittances as well as the technical terms refer only to transactions between residents and nonresidents of a compiling economy. For quick reference, the *RCG* includes a glossary of remittances-related terminology (Appendix 1).

[1]The Centre for Latin American Monetary Studies (CEMLA), an association of Latin American and Caribbean central banks, has developed a separate compilation guide on remittances for its member countries. This effort was undertaken as part of a joint project on remittances with the Multilateral Investment Fund of the Inter-American Development Bank. The CEMLA compilation guide is more prescriptive than the *RCG* because it promotes a standardized compilation methodology for member countries based on the use of transactions reporting by banks and direct reporting by money transfer operators. The CEMLA guide also is more oriented to receiver countries, whereas the *RCG* is oriented toward both sending and receiving countries.

CHAPTER

2 Understanding Remittances: Demography, Transaction Channels, and Regulatory Aspects

2.1. Cross-border remittances are a challenge to measure because they are heterogeneous, with numerous small transactions conducted by individuals through a large variety of channels. Prerequisites to improving data on remittances are an understanding of the transaction channels that are available and an ability to compile or estimate data that cover all channels that are heavily used. The transaction channels used may depend on the financial system, the overall institutional environment of the sending and receiving countries, the convenience and costs associated with use of these channels, and the demographic characteristic of the senders and receivers.

2.2. Remittances are often linked to migration. Migration is the movement of persons from one economy to another. As used in the *RCG* and in the balance of payments more generally, "migrant" refers to a person who emigrates from an economy of origin and becomes a resident in another economy. It should be noted, however, that migration status is not relevant to the definitions of standard components in *BPM6*.

2.3. A person may move from one economy to another for the purpose of short-term employment. In the *RCG*, a "short-term worker" refers to a person who moves to another economy for the purpose of employment on a short-term (less than one year) basis.[2] Short-term workers and migrants supporting relatives in their country of origin are a major source of cross-border remittance flows. This chapter discusses the link between different types of workers and their associated remittance flows.

2.4. The identification of transaction channels for remittances can help compilers assess the extent to which their existing data sources cover remittance transactions. Remittances can take various forms, ranging from funds transferred through "formal" or regulated institutions or channels (e.g., banks, nonbank financial institutions, and money transfer operators) to "semi-formal" and "informal" channels (e.g., hawala, cash carried in person, in-kind transfers).

2.5. The *RCG* does not strictly identify which transaction channels qualify as formal or informal, recognizing that such judgments are subject to country-specific legal, regulatory, and institutional factors and therefore may vary from country to country. The *RCG* also emphasizes that all international transactions, no matter whether they are informal or formal, legal or illegal, should be covered by balance of payments statistics. However, at various points the *RCG* refers to the difficulties in obtaining data on informal remittance transactions. It has been argued that, because of such difficulties, the remittance transactions undertaken through informal channels are sometimes not well covered in current balance of payments data.

2.6. Section A of this chapter provides a demographic perspective on remittances, looking at the relationship between movement of persons for short-term or long-term employment purposes and remittances. Section B develops an inventory of transaction channels and their institutional environment, which is vital for understanding remittance flows and potential data sources. Section C draws attention to the divergent legal and regulatory environments of remittance transactions by individual countries and the widespread use of informal channels.

A. Demographic Perspective on Remittances

2.7. International labor migration has attracted attention in the discussions of reasons for increasing international trade in services and demographic shifts observable in many parts of the world. The roots of

[2]Also includes border workers.

cross-border labor migration are related to, among other factors, divergences in economic performance between countries and regions, uneven technological change, and the integration of markets and societies.[3]

2.8. Following the skill content of labor, migrants and short-term workers can be categorized as unskilled, low-skilled, and skilled. Because the migration of low-skilled workers is generally associated with stiff immigration restrictions, there is a tendency for illegal or unregulated migration of unskilled or low-skilled workers. The extent of the informal economy in the host country affects the demand for illegal labor. In a comparative sense, a deficit of skilled workers in the host countries results in a less restrictive regime for skilled workers and as a result skilled migrants and short-term workers tend to flow through the legal channel. Because skilled migrants and short-term workers are more likely to migrate through legal channels, they reduce the administrative burden of the destination countries in enforcing migration regulations. There has been a steady increase in the migration of skilled workers from developing to developed countries since the 1970s. It is argued that although skilled migrants and short-term workers tend to have opportunities under unilateral visa programs, unskilled migrants and short-term workers usually depend on bilateral or regional agreements such as seasonal and other work programs.

2.9. Numerous demographic characteristics are thought to be associated with remittances, and there is general agreement on the effect of many of these variables on the amounts remitted. These characteristics include size of the stock of migrants and short-term workers, country of origin and work, ethnic background, duration of stay, average income level, gender, legal status, and the presence of children in the household.[4] Income is recognized as the primary determinant of the capacity to remit.

2.10. Although the motivation of migrants to remit declines with the duration of stay, their capacity to remit often increases because their income tends to rise over time. Such statistics are useful for understanding the dynamics underlying remittance flows, but they are scarcely available in most countries. The migration statistics are generally collected through a population register or population census.[5] The immigration data of countries with population registers are generally more accurate than those of countries without a register or census, because registration with the authorities is often necessary for migrants and short-term workers to obtain, for instance, a job, a dwelling, or health insurance. However, the issue of whether the emigration data of register countries are more accurate than those of census countries is not settled.

2.11. The problems in obtaining data arise in contiguous countries where the percentage of seasonal or illegal workers tends to be high. Because the illegal workers stay away from either the population census or the network of the formal modes of transfer out of fear of apprehension by the authorities (associated with the fact they are in the country illegally), it becomes challenging to correctly gauge the size of the stock of migrants and short-term workers. Depending on circumstances in individual countries, it may be important to develop an integrated approach to estimation that involves coordinated efforts of migration authorities, immigration offices, enumerators for the population census, and compilers of remittances statistics (migration data are further discussed in Box 2.1).

2.12. A worker may travel for either short-term or long-term employment, partly depending on the socioeconomic and political conditions in the host and the source countries. In most instances, short-term workers consume less of their income than do migrants, and therefore more of their income or compensation is available to support family members in their home country. Short-term workers maintain strong ties with their country of origin because of their permanent interest in their home countries. Among migrants, remittance senders tend to be more concentrated among more recently arrived immigrants, and at least half the

[3]Migration is, of course, not a recent phenomenon. However, the past 50 years saw rapid improvements in transportation and financial infrastructure that allowed short-term workers to travel even longer distances in search of work and migrants to remain in touch with their country of origin, such as through visits and lower-cost communication, and to more easily transfer funds such as remittances.

[4]More specifically, gender affects the level of income of the migrants and short-term workers because females often have lower average incomes than males. The presence of children in the household increases household expenditures and changes the nature of economic interest, and therefore reduces the propensity to remit. Research conducted by Statistics Canada showed that the proportion of migrants and short-term workers remitting and the amounts remitted were different depending on place of birth.

[5]Countries with population registers require residents to register their primary residence, and to provide administrative data on demographic variables. Some countries maintain a registration requirement but also carry out a population census; such countries often rely primarily on registration for understanding demographic change. Other countries rely solely on population censuses.

Box 2.1. Data on Migration

Data sources for compiling migration statistics include population censuses, surveys, border surveys, and other administrative records. However, reliable statistics on migration are difficult to collect and are often incomplete. Annual data on bilateral migrant stocks (migrants and short-term workers), for instance, are available for only a few Organization for Economic Cooperation and Development (OECD) countries. Many countries collect data on migrant stocks using population censuses, which are usually infrequent, and estimates of growth rates are needed to produce time-series data. A further problem is that individual countries may apply different definitions to classify the data, leading to data that are incomparable. For example, differences occur in the way countries classify migrants and short-term workers according to their duration of stay and the purpose of their visit. Also, many countries use the place of birth of a migrant or short-term worker as a key variable in migration statistics, but some countries use the concept of nationality, and a small number of countries use a combination of the two. These definitions are not compatible with the concept of residence as it is used in balance of payments and national accounts statistics.

Sources: World Bank (2008a and 2008b).

migrants who have stayed for up to 10 years may be regular remitters.[6]

2.13. Compared with migrants, short-term workers are associated with lower fiscal burden on the host country, less social conflict, and greater flexibility of host countries to adjust labor inflows in accordance with the domestic labor market conditions.

2.14. Migration programs for labor may promote more legal flows of labor. Bilateral labor agreements have proved to be important in facilitating the migration of low-skilled and seasonal workers (these agreements often encourage migration by reducing the regulatory burden; high-skilled labor often is mobile independently of bilateral agreements).

2.15. Whereas employment of short-term workers may not involve movement of families, migration is often associated with movement of families along with workers, perhaps with some time lag. Migration may also entail some degree of reduction in labor participation rates because the families (spouse and children) of migrants may not fully participate in the labor force in the host country, depending on their skill and age characteristics.

[6]Although remittances are related to migrations, an important distinction must be made between the immigrants and the remitters. Remitters are, in part, a subset of immigrants; also, some nonmigrants remit.

B. Inventory of Transaction Channels and Institutional Environment

2.16. This section provides an inventory of transaction channels used for remittances and briefly discusses the impact the institutional environment has on the availability of transaction channels and their selection. It considers both formal and informal channels and attempts to identify new channels, such as Internet and cell phone-based transactions.

2.17. The channels are not strictly identified as formal or informal. The reason is that a particular channel may be viewed differently based on the regulatory regime, institutional structure, and legal system in different countries. A specific channel may be formal in one country but informal in another, given its regulatory treatment. Also, the inventory presented here should not be considered complete because remittance service providers innovate quickly and new transaction channels may be developed.

2.18. As noted, money remittance transaction may involve a sender, a recipient, intermediaries in both countries, and the payment interface used by the intermediaries; together, these comprise the remittance channel (see Figure 2.1). Most remittances are of relatively low value, are regular or frequent, and mainly involve persons at both ends because they are generally targeted at family maintenance. Remittances assume the form of cash or credit transfers and transfers in kind (involving transfers of goods). Cash transfers are

Figure 2.1. Remittance Channels

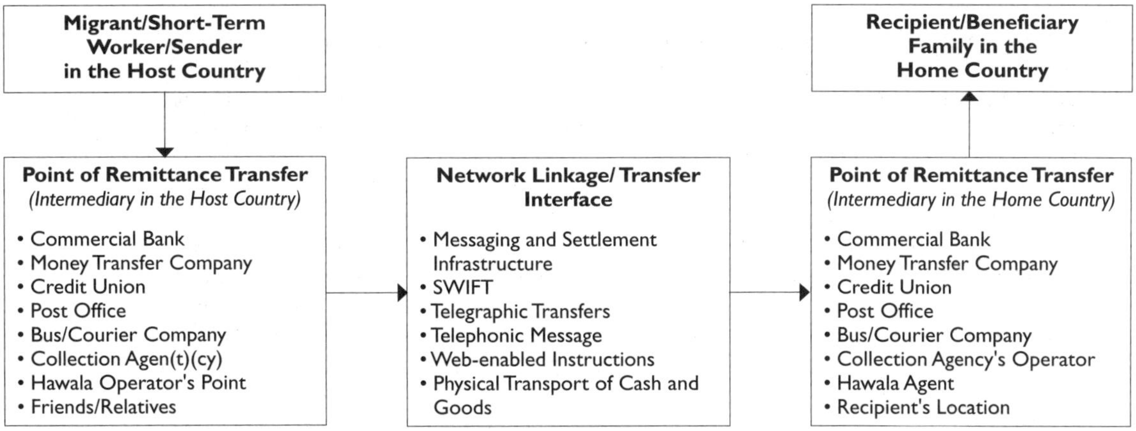

Note: Not all funds transferred through these channels are remittances.

sent in either the foreign currency or the local currency by means of physical transfer of cash. Credit transfers are based on payment instructions from providers in the sending country to providers in the receiving country. The payment instructions using messaging services enable contact between the entities operating at the sending and the receiving ends, and the settlement process enables actual transfer of funds between these entities. Noncash or in-kind transfers, which comprise mainly consumer goods, involve physical delivery predominantly through informal routes. However, before a look at the microstructure of the channels used for cross-border transfer of funds by migrants and short-term workers, it would be appropriate to understand broadly how the remittance transactions take place. A remittance transaction typically requires some type of network to connect senders and receivers for the purpose of messaging and settlement of funds.

2.19. Cross-border remittance flows can take place through various channels, depending on the availability of services, preference of the remitter, and the institutional environment. Formal remittance channels are those officially authorized to operate in the money transfer business, such as banks, money transfer operators, or other officially registered institutions. Semiformal remittance channels include formal institutions providing money transfer services outside the regulatory mechanisms of the country authorities. These institutions are well organized in transferring money but not controlled by any financial services regulatory authority. Informal remittance channels are outside of financial regulation and supervision but often legal; the least official and formal channels for transfer of funds may involve intermediaries who do not operate as formal businesses. The remitter's choice between the various channels of fund transfers may be influenced by a host of factors, such as the kind of institutional infrastructure available in the host and the home countries, ease of access to formal financial institutions, speed of funds transfer through alternate channels, differential cost of funds transfer, government regulations, incentives offered by the home country in the form of tax concessions and interest rates, identification requirements, and procedural burdens embedded in the formal channels. These issues are discussed in later sections.

2.20. The relative attractiveness of the various channels of transfers is determined by a multitude of factors. A high level of penetration of the formal banking sector in the sending and receiving countries may encourage migrants and short-term workers to use account-to-account transfers. However, despite the availability of bank services, fixed transaction costs and burdensome documentation requirements to meet regulatory obligations may render small-value transactions unattractive for the banks and clients. Thus, the cost of sending money abroad may significantly influence the choice between formal and informal channels.

2.21. In addition to costs, speed of delivery may strongly influence the decision of the sender to choose a particular channel. Although online methods offered by formal channels are relatively more efficient in terms of delivery speed, their usage is constrained by the lack of information technology infrastructure at the sender's or the receiver's location. Informal channels also can be efficient in delivery speed; it is often reported that transfer through hawala takes less than 12 hours to reach the recipient.

2.22. Apart from explicit costs, hidden costs in foreign exchange transactions may significantly influence decisions regarding a particular channel. For instance, exchange rates offered may significantly change the final payout to the recipient and hence the attractiveness of a particular mode of transfer. In particular, under exchange control regimes, unofficial operators may offer a currency exchange rate that is more favorable than the official exchange rate, attracting senders to informal channels. Risk of losing money in transit may also influence the choice of a particular channel. Where migrants and short-term workers are able to frequently visit their home country, they may prefer to carry cash or deliver goods themselves or have their friends make delivery. Migration status may also significantly affect the attractiveness of a particular channel. Illegal migrants and short-term workers may prefer to remit money through informal channels because they may not meet identification requirements to open bank accounts and remit money. Furthermore, formal channels are also more likely to be used when the geographical distance between the sending and receiving countries is high, causing difficulty in physically transferring remittances in cash or kind. However, some informal channels are effective and popular in making long-distance payments.

2.23. The various formats of fund transfer that may be used by the migrants and short-term workers are set out below.

Banking channel

2.24. Commercial banks are traditionally important vehicles for effecting cross-border remittance transactions, in light of their extensive networks in both the sending and the receiving countries, and participation in the international payments and settlement systems. Some banks with a global presence may use their own network for money transfers, whereas others with limited networks may use a franchise transfer service provided by a global operator, join a cooperative network, or utilize a correspondent banking relationship. The international banking network—interlinking national payment systems—enables remittances from a bank providing fund transfer facilities to be transferred to any other bank across the globe.[7]

2.25. The payment formats used by banks include electronic fund transfers and transfers by telegram, fax, and telephone. Types of fund transfers through banks may be cash transfers, account-to-account transfers, prepaid funds (prepaid cards, money orders, bankers' drafts), and credit (credit cards). The type of transfer most often used is telegraphic or other wire transfers that operate on the basis of the branch network or the correspondent relationship. The remittance is sent by a bank via wire transfer to its branch or correspondent bank in the beneficiary country, which forwards the remittance electronically or by draft to the beneficiary bank. Checks can be deposited for credit to a beneficiary's account. Drafts can be purchased from exchange companies or the correspondent bank and mailed to the branch where the beneficiary has an account.

2.26. Online money transfer services offered by banks are an efficient means of fund transfers and enable cross-border transfers from the sender's bank account to the beneficiary's account in the receiving country. These are more often used in remittance corridors where a banking network is well developed and correspondent relationships are widely used.[8] Innovations in information technology and the introduction of increasingly sophisticated methods of fund transfers, such as dual debit cards, stored value cards, and other variants of card-based online transfers, also are now being used with increasing frequency in many countries.

2.27. The automated teller machine (ATM) card is widely used as a remittance channel. A credit or debit card product uses credit and debit card payment systems for transferring money from one card account to another. Such transfers often involve the deposit of the funds into a card account with a given bank branch and subsequent transfer of the funds to another card issued by the same branch held by persons in the receiving country. This two-ATM model is used in Latin America, with a remitter based in the United States sending a second card with full rights to withdraw funds to a

[7]In some countries there exist bilateral agreements for the settlement of transactions channeled through the banking system with the involvement of central banks. For example, the program Directo Mexico transfers funds between the United States and Mexico with the involvement of the Bank of Mexico and the United States Federal Reserve.

[8]A remittance corridor is the path connecting a specific pair of countries or a specific pair of cities between which international remittances flow (CEMLA).

family member who can use the card at ATMs abroad. These products are also available in South Africa but have not been widely promoted. They require a relatively strong level of cooperation and trust between both parties. Also, limited ATM infrastructure in many countries restricts the availability of this method.

2.28. Technology support providers offer their Internet interface to banks, which may then be integrated to the bank's website. A customer subsequently wishing to transfer funds would log on to the bank website and interactively direct a transfer of funds. The system debits the customer's overseas bank account and credits the account of the receiving bank/service provider for credits to the beneficiary's account, as per instructions given by the customer.

2.29. Banks may also undertake money transfer through a variety of innovative arrangements with the financial entities in the host country. For instance, Indian banks have entered into special arrangements with private exchange houses in the Middle East, Singapore, and Hong Kong SAR for channeling inward remittances. Under this arrangement, an exchange house issues drafts (in Indian currency) to the beneficiary and at the end of each day calculates total drawings. On the next working day, daily collections are deposited in a designated account opened in the name of the drawee bank by the exchange house with a bank acceptable to the drawee bank.

Money transfer operators

2.30. Money transfer operators (MTOs) are financial companies (but usually not banks) engaged in cross-border transfer of funds using either their internal system or access to another cross-border banking network.[9] MTOs may use their own outlets or numerous transfer agents, such as banks, exchange bureaus, post offices, and other intermediaries like retail outlets, cell phone centers, travel agencies, drug stores, and gas stations, to deliver remittances in the destination country, because MTOs and associated activities usually address the same target clients. Funds are delivered through cash, checks, or drafts. MTOs have wide networks in the sending and receiving countries, have less stringent identification requirements, and often focus on low-value, high-frequency transactions. To send or receive money at an agent's location does not require credit cards, bank accounts, memberships, or citizenship papers. The payments, in the large majority of cases, are carried out by collecting cash from a sending party and delivering cash to a receiving party (cash-to-cash).

2.31. The remittance process through an MTO often begins with a sender delivering cash to a subagent of the MTO in the host country. Second, the subagent transfers funds to the MTO agent through the domestic payments system. In the third step, the MTO agent orders its bank to transfer funds from its domestic account to the overseas account of a partner, nonresident MTO agent. Once the funds are credited to its account, the partner MTO agent requests that funds be credited to its subagent. The subagent in the receiving country then, in a final step, delivers cash to the final beneficiary. This chain involves somewhat fewer steps when banks operate as MTO subagents.

2.32. MTOs are quite varied in their size, organizational structure, and procedures. Global MTOs work mainly on the principle of franchised services.[10] Such MTOs rely on a proprietary network, representing the infrastructure of their payment systems, which allows a cost-effective interconnection of a large number of offices spread worldwide. A global MTO network includes agents, subagents, and clearing centers.

2.33. Subagents represent the operational front office or the access point or "physical counter" that migrants, short-term workers, and other clients approach to send or receive funds internationally. A large number of subagents all over the world provide MTOs with a strong presence in almost all countries. The subagents settle with their parent agent the net balance of amounts they received from sender clients and amounts they paid to recipient clients. This first level of clearing occurs frequently, such as on a daily basis, and is normally carried out through a (domestic) bank transfer.

2.34. The agents, under varied legal arrangements, work on behalf of the MTO's parent company. They can be considered the operational back-office units,

[9]In some countries, MTOs are required to be registered with monetary authorities as nonbank financial institutions, whereas in others they operate as companies outside the financial sector. Very few countries allow only banks to operate as MTOs (in these cases, domestic banks acquire franchises of international MTO chains).

[10]CPSS and World Bank (2006) defines a franchised service where a central provider, without necessarily having any access points of its own, provides a proprietary service: the central provider creates infrastructure to support the service (e.g., messaging and settlement, advertising) and obtains the necessary access points by inviting institutions in both sending and receiving countries to offer the service or act as franchisees on essentially standardized terms.

because they carry out a relevant part of the administrative work—in particular, collecting details on outgoing payments from subagents and transmitting the details on incoming payments to subagents. Therefore, agent information systems must store and maintain detailed administrative records on payments, such as the subagent involved, amount transferred, fees, date of transaction, and country and address of the sender and the beneficiary. As a consequence, agents may be a potentially valuable statistical data source.

2.35. The agent is engaged in a second level of clearing, perhaps once a week or bimonthly, to settle the aggregate net balance of remittance activities—that is, the sum of balances of the agent vis-à-vis its subagents—with the international clearing center. In addition to sending or receiving funds, agents also exchange with the clearing center all information needed to identify outbound and inward payments. The clearing center may be located in a country that is not the sending or receiving country, nor the country of the MTO's parent company.

2.36. The exchange of funds between subagents, agents, and the clearing center requires the intermediation of banks. Whenever the settlement involves two different countries—this happens often for transfers between agents and the clearing center—a cross-border bank transfer occurs, typically through correspondent banking relationships. The clearing center takes care of the multilateral clearing of flows in various directions, ensuring appropriate funding of agents in receiving countries. Settlements, even if on a net basis, are always channeled through the banking system.[11]

2.37. The money transfer industry is characterized by the presence of small- to medium-sized MTO firms, which do not rely on a proprietary network. Usually such MTOs transact in cash with clients and transfer or receive the corresponding amounts abroad through the intermediation of the banking system. Although the global MTO subagent that anticipates receiving money may grant a sort of short-term credit to beneficiaries before receiving the actual credit, for nonglobal MTOs cash is delivered to beneficiaries mainly only after the bank transfers related to the payment are completed. A special contractual arrangement is usually in place to regulate the relationship between small MTOs and the settlement bank used to transfer funds abroad.

2.38. In the case of large MTOs, transfers are made virtually everywhere, even the most remote locations, almost through a "door-to-door" delivery of money. The persons operating MTO subagencies are often of the same nationality as potential customers and speak the same language. This situation involves some "ethnic proximity," which potential customers would find attractive.[12] Newly arrived immigrants are characterized by a relatively low rate of financial participation in the host country and, for this reason, by a relatively high propensity to use MTO services. This explains the higher success of this channel in countries that represent relatively new migration destinations. The share of MTOs is also high when the banks and the informal channels, for any reason, are less popular. The usefulness of the MTO data as a statistical source varies across countries depending on volume of transactions, quality of data, and other factors.

Postal network

2.39. Post offices, traditionally the agents of domestic money transfers, have also emerged as important carriers of cross-border funds and are generally regulated by communications laws in most countries and not by the central banks. Post offices either provide their own services for international money transfer or act as agents for other money transfer companies.[13] International postal money order service is available to transfer funds to individuals or firms in countries that have entered into agreements. Among the remittance service providers, post offices have the largest outreach network including remote locations, particularly in receiving developing countries where the financial infrastructure is inadequate to deliver remittances.

2.40. Remittance can easily be made to a number of countries from post offices handling international remittance services. International postal money orders may be sent by letter mail or expedited mail service.

[11]It may therefore be incorrect to argue that traditional data collection systems based on bank reports completely miss covering remittances through MTOs. However, settlements may obscure flows because they are routed through international settlement centers and typically are made on a net basis. Chapter 4 provides further detail.

[12]For example, in sender countries, MTO subagents are often located in ethnic stores selling goods originating from immigrants' home countries.

[13]The United States Post Office has its own transfer system, Dinero Seguro (safe money), which began in 1997 and offers electronic money transfer. In Europe, the Euro-Giro system operates in direct cooperation with European postal systems in international money transfers to more than 30 countries, including China, Israel, and Brazil. In Africa, PostSpeed is operated by post offices in Uganda, Tanzania, and Kenya for fund delivery within East Africa.

However, money orders to some countries can be mailed directly by the remitter. Usually there are limits on the maximum amount for a single postal money order. Ordinary money orders, in which the remittance amount and handling charges are paid at the post office in cash or via a transfer from the remitter's account, are available for delivery to the payee's address.

2.41. Even though the postal network covers all areas of the world, it has not been fully utilized in cross-border transfer of remittances in many countries because of limits on transactions, liquidity problems in the disbursing outlets in the receiving countries, and delays. In some developing countries, money transfer agencies use a postal network to enhance their outreach in remittance transfer markets.

Credit unions

2.42. Many credit unions facilitate international payments by providing bank drafts and, in some cases, immediate electronic money transfers through agency arrangements with large international MTOs.[14] Credit unions usually arrange money transfers through either an existing network or the International Remittance Network (IRnet), a remittance settlement platform established by the World Council of Credit Unions.[15] Through it, credit unions offer an electronic funds transfer service providing credit union members with a way to send money overseas or domestically.

2.43. Under IRnet, transactions are processed through an automated clearing house facility, whereby funds are transferred to an intermediary bank with whom the credit union has an arrangement. The bank in turn transfers funds to its branch in the recipient country and credits the account of the credit union.

Telecommunications companies

2.44. Telephone companies have recently started to offer remittance services in many countries, often using their mobile phone networks for making transactions. These services are designed so that the recipient can receive credit for prepaid telecommunication services ("air time credit") for their relatives or obtain cash. Prepaid credit is intended for payment for telephone services and often cannot be sold (or refunded). Therefore, these transfers are practical only up to the amounts that the recipient would be required to pay for telephone usage. Stored value cards issued by mobile phone companies are one means of transferring money by individuals using mobile phones. Under this arrangement, a telecommunications service provider requires the subscriber to register with the system.

2.45. An example of the use of telecommunications companies for remittances is the case of the Philippines, where two mobile telephone companies have recently introduced mobile phone-based money transfer services. The recipient receives a text message confirming the transfer and withdraws cash through any authorized agent. This is a means to make a cash-to-cash transfer when neither party holds a bank account. Similar transfer mechanisms are being planned in West Africa and elsewhere.

2.46. Another variant is the mobile phone payment system based on Subscriber Identity Module (SIM) technology, available in Zambia and the Democratic Republic of the Congo. The sender can deposit funds into an account by using a cell phone to transfer funds from a bank account or deposit cash at a partner bank. Purchases can be made through text messaging by entering into the phone the amount to be paid and authenticating the transaction using a personal identification number. The service provider instantly transfers the amount to the merchant's account.

2.47. The rate of innovation in this field is high, and new remittance services based on mobile phones are announced regularly. An example of a mobile phone–based system is outlined in Box 2.2.

2.48. Money transfer services based on mobile phones are gaining popularity because they transmit money "at the speed of text" and are cheap and relatively secure. It is also worth noting that mobile remittances draw a large portion of the informal remittances into the banking system as financial services become available to the unbanked community.

Internet

2.49. The Internet is also being used as a means to transfer funds between households. Some "traditional" MTOs offer Internet-based transactions in addition to transactions through their branches and agents. Other companies are based on Internet-only business models.

[14]Credit unions have been active in funds transfer particularly in the United States-Latin American corridor.

[15]IRnet provides service to more than 40 countries in Latin America, Asia, Africa, and Europe.

Box 2.2. An Example of the Flow of Information and Funds in a Telephone-Based Remittance System

Information Flow

A sender visits a remittance company and fills out an information sheet. The remittance company in the sender's country submits to its partner bank in the recipient's country all relevant information provided by the sender. At the same time, the remittance company assigns an account number to the beneficiary's mobile phone and credits the number of the beneficiary. The service sends a text message to both the sender and the recipient, notifying them that the money has been transferred. The beneficiary can now get cash from the partnering institutions or through an ATM at a participating bank.

Funds Flow

The remittance company in the sender's country maintains a prefunded account at a local bank in the receiving country. When a sender remits, the funds are transferred to the beneficiary's money card. Meanwhile, the beneficiary receives a notification through a text message that the funds are credited to his or her money card. The beneficiary then claims his or her cash at accredited encashment centers by showing the text message in his or her mobile phone.

2.50. Personal money transfers from one virtual account to another have recently entered the market and are quite innovative. Although these payments are not widespread, they have become more popular. In order to make a transfer, a person opens a virtual account on the Internet. Money is put on the account usually using express payment cards, cash dispensers, cash offices of credit organizations, or credit cards. Money on virtual account is electronic money (stored value or prepaid product in which a record of the funds or value available to the consumer for multipurpose use is stored on an electronic device in the consumer's possession).[16] Cross-border money transfers can flow between virtual personal accounts. If a person intends to make a payment via the Internet, it will be sufficient to put money on virtual account and transfer money to another account through the electronic payment system. Recipients of transferred funds exchange electronic money for national currency, or could put it on their account at a local bank. Electronic money systems are managed by firms that are considered credit organizations but that operate under simplified rules compared with banks.

Courier companies

2.51. The entry of courier services in the remittance transfer market has been attributed to the weaknesses of other formal institutions. Courier companies may deliver remittances through regular mail, electronic communications, and their own physical delivery of packages. At the remitting end, the transaction involves the sender visiting the location of the courier company and tendering the money. The courier company receives information about both the sender and the receiver. At the receiving end, an employee or agent of the courier company visits the recipient and delivers the money after proper identification of the recipient.

Transport operators

2.52. Cross-border transport operators (primarily bus courier operators) are involved in carrying goods and money. Bus courier operators are not official money transfer agents, but they may transport declared or undeclared money as part of their legitimate courier business. The transaction involves the sender visiting the bus company office and tendering the cash over the counter. The sender, in turn, is given a receipt and a password, which he or she shares with the beneficiary in the receiving country. To collect the money from the bus company office, the beneficiary provides the password and personal identification, as required.

2.53. The use of cross-border transport operators as a channel of sending both cash remittances and non-cash remittances (in-kind transfers, mainly durable consumer goods) is substantial in African countries, such as Kenya, Tanzania, and Uganda.[17] They have

[16]For a more detailed description of electronic money, see CPSS (2004).

[17]Between South Africa and Zimbabwe, cross-border transport *(continued)*

Table 2.1. Informal Value Transfer Systems

Type of Transfer	Transfer Mechanism	Where It Is Popular	Cash Flow Between Countries at Time of Transfer
Hawala	"Transfer": payment instruction transmitted	Middle East, South Asia	No
Fei Ch'ien	"Flying money": payment instruction transmitted	Asia	No
Hundi	"Collect": payment instruction transmitted	Asia, Middle East	No
Chits and chops	"Notes, seals": payment instruction transmitted	Asia	No
Black market peso exchange	Asset exchange	Latin America	No
Cross-border transport operators/drivers	Physical transfers	Africa	Yes
Relatives, friends, migrants, and short-term workers traveling home	Physical transfers	Middle East, Asia, Europe, Africa, Latin America	Yes

Sources: El Qorchi, Maimbo, and Wilson (2003); and U.K. Remittance Working Group (2005).
Note: Informal fund transfers are also known as hui kuan (Hong Kong SAR), padala (Philippines), and phei kwan (Thailand).

gained importance because of the inherent advantage of this mode in terms of speed and cost vis-à-vis formal methods, and convenience in delivery.

Other, often unregulated, channels

2.54. A large number of small money transfer businesses all over the world are often not subject to registration, licensing, or regulation, depending on local circumstances. Many of these businesses are part of channels that are culturally embedded and have been described as "alternative remittance systems," "informal value transfer systems," and "informal funds transfer systems" (see Table 2.1).

2.55. Initially developed to facilitate trade between countries (and sometimes regions within countries), these channels later emerged as inexpensive and effective methods to transfer money to remote locations. They are popular for small-value transactions by migrants and short-term workers, although they are not always as secure as more formal alternatives. Tighter regulatory requirements (such as anti–money laundering and combating the financing of terrorism legislation) have tended to increase the requirements for opening accounts and thus discourage the use of banks by low-value remittance customers.

2.56. Exchange control restrictions create a wedge between the official exchange rate and the black market rate. These restrictions thereby essentially impose a penalty on migrants and short-term workers who remit funds through the official channel and contribute to the relative attractiveness of using informal channels. However, timely delivery of funds vis-à-vis the formal channels and in some cases delivery by agents to the doorstep of the recipient make these channels attractive.

2.57. Illegal migrants and short-term workers (who in some countries do not have access to the regulated money transfer system because of identification requirements) often prefer informal channels because these are unregulated. Nonetheless, the use of unregulated channels appears to have diminished in recent years as a result of the liberalization of foreign exchange controls, reforms in the payments infrastructure, and competition in the remittance market.[18] Reliable data and information on unregulated remittances channels are lacking.

2.58. Among the informal value transfer channels to developing countries, hawala is apparently the most organized system in the Middle East and South Asia (Figure 2.2). Hawala transactions go through a special-

operators are the mode of channeling both cash and goods most preferred by migrants (Maphosa, 2005).

[18]However, in some countries, such as Haiti, Cuba, and Nicaragua, unregulated remittance channels account for more than 50 percent of the total funds transferred (Orozco, 2004).

Figure 2.2. Structure of Hawala Value Chain

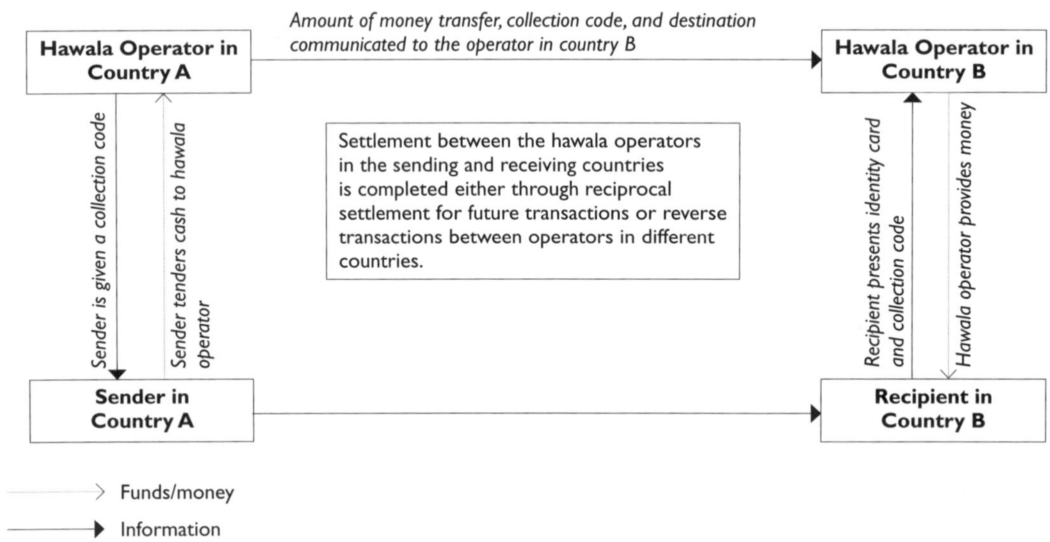

ist broker. Money itself does not regularly move across borders, either electronically or physically, except to settle net positions. That is, the system is based on trust and the brokers balance the transfers over time.

2.59. A typical transaction involves the sender visiting the hawala operator in the sending country (A). Hawala operators may operate from locations such as grocery stores or travel companies. Basically, the hawala operator in country A receives money from the sender and advises (through telephone call, fax, e-mail, and so forth) the counterpart hawala operator in the receiving country (B) to disburse the cash to the beneficiary in local currency after proper identification and verifying the remittance code (password) from the beneficiary. Subsequently the transactions need to be settled between the hawala operators of countries A and B, bilaterally or multilaterally (involving a hawala operator in a third country).

2.60. Networking among hawala operators is required for the smooth operation of the system. The settlement may assume many variants of the reverse transactions between hawala operators in different countries. Operators in the hawala networks often rely on modern telecommunication technologies and may use complex arrangements to settle transactions.

2.61. Another informal value transfer channel is hundi. Even though hawala and hundi are used as interchangeable terms in parts of South Asia, they differ. Hundi was one of the earliest and most important credit instruments in India. Thus, unlike hawala, a hundi is a physical document or financial instrument. It could be used for transferring remittances (the confusion with hawala arises from this point) or as a bill of exchange. In simple terms, it was a popular bearer instrument. According to a study, hundis also could be used as finance bills or trade bills. The hundi was payable either on sight or at a later date. In some countries, such as Pakistan and Bangladesh, the term used to describe the practice of hawala is actually *hundi*.

2.62. Technically, a hundi is an unconditional order in writing made by a person directing another to pay a certain sum of money to another person. In a typical hundi transaction, the migrant or short-term worker transfers a sum of foreign currency to a local agent under the agreement that the overseas moneychanger of that agent transfer the local currency equivalent at an agreed exchange rate to the sender's family or nominee. Hundi dealers offer door-to-door and same-day service, which is particularly welcome in remote areas.

2.63. In the chit[19] system, which was introduced by the British colonialists in China during the nineteenth

[19]Chit is a diminutive of the Hindi word *chitti* and means a note, pass, or certificate given to a servant.

century, the salaries of workers employed by the British were deposited to an escrow account managed by a Chinese comprador (an intermediary between a European firm and a local buyer). These foreign workers would write chits to pay for food and other essentials that they purchased from local merchants. In turn, the merchants would present these chits for collection (payment) to the comprador, who would then deduct the corresponding amounts from the accounts of the foreign workers.

2.64. A system similar to the chit system is called chop; it works in the same way as the hawala system and is still in use today. A client in country A wishing to remit money to a recipient in country B goes to a broker at a store or outlet who will take the cash, make an entry into a ledger book for the amount received, and communicate the relevant information about the transaction (amount to be remitted, name and location of recipient, and so forth) to his or her counterpart broker in country B. The broker also creates a chop (in this situation, possibly a train ticket or playing card), tears it into two pieces, gives one piece to the client, and sends the other piece to the overseas counterpart. The client sends his or her half of the chop to the recipient. A match of the two halves must be made before the broker releases the money to the recipient.

2.65. In some remittance transaction models, aggregated financial claims are offset (and settled) by transactions in goods. This model does not require cross-border financial settlements and is therefore popular in countries with foreign exchange restrictions. One example is the black market peso exchange, a form of asset swap used in South American countries. A migrant or short-term worker wishing to transfer money to his or her home country submits funds to a broker, who agrees to pay out an equivalent amount to the intended recipients in the remitter's home country (the broker has offices or representatives in both the remitter's host country and home country). In countries where foreign exchange restrictions make access to foreign currency (and imported goods) scarce, this equivalent amount may be based on a discount to the official rate. More specifically, the broker uses funds from the remitter to purchase goods in the remitter's host country, and ships these goods to importers in the remitter's home country. The importers pay the broker representative for the imported goods using local currency. The broker representative, in turn, pays the intended recipient of the remittances.

2.66. The "cash-in-hand" mode of transfer is popular particularly in remittance corridors where there are constraints in accessing formal financial institutions, as well as in congruous regions where migrants and short-term workers frequently travel back and forth to their home country and thereby can reduce the risk of nondelivery of remittances to beneficiaries.[20] Many migrants and short-term workers use a courier system, which involves a regularly driven van from the host or home countries (and back) to move goods and funds. Carrying cash (whether by friends, relatives, or migrants/short-term workers themselves) while traveling between the host country and the home country is a popular mode of fund transfers in many African and Latin American countries.[21]

2.67. Cash-intensive businesses, particularly outlets with good international communication facilities, often offer remittance transfer services as a sideline. Such businesses include foreign exchange outlets, unregulated financial houses, shipping companies, grocery businesses, brokers, jewelers, gold dealers, clothing shops, guest houses, restaurants, travel agents, phone cards, international telephone shops, bus companies, and taxi firms. Country case studies show that churches and other religious organizations also often play a role in fund-raising or funds transfer to the place of origin. Usually this is linked to community projects, but a modest role in transferring individual remittances is sometimes also reported. Nongovernmental organizations could also raise money and transport humanitarian aid to the home areas.

Trade-based systems

2.68. In trade-based remittance systems, the remittance senders finance the purchases of imported goods by traders who reside in the same country as the remittance recipient. The traders use earnings from the sales of these goods to pay remittances to the designated beneficiaries.

2.69. One of the most common trade-based remittance methods is based on a credit system. The remittance sender contacts an importer in the recipient country (typically the sender's country of origin) with the request to pay out funds to the beneficiary based on credit. After the arrangement has been made, the

[20]In-kind transfers are popular in many African countries, particularly among migrants and short-term workers from rural areas.

[21]In Cuba, the informal system of mulas is widely used to carry cash and goods by informal entrepreneurs from the United States, who visit regularly as tourists. A survey of African migrants in the United Kingdom conducted by Africarecruit in 2003 estimated that 36 percent made use of the cash-in-hand transfer method.

importer pays the agreed amount of money to the recipient. The arrangements could be made in person (if the importer visits the sending country) or by telephone, fax, or Internet. The remittance sender will repay the loan when the importer next visits the country where the sender lives.

2.70. In another version of this system, remittance senders make advance deposits with the importers, who will pay out funds to the recipients at a later point in time. In this version, the importer will accept deposits from senders during a business trip to another country. During this trip, the importer may then use the funds received to purchase goods. Subsequently, the goods are imported to the country of the remittance recipients and sold there; the revenue is used to pay cash remittances.

2.71. Both versions of the trade-based remittance system are often used by migrants and short-term workers from small countries that have a strong link with another country (e.g., Swaziland imports many goods from South Africa, and many Swazi nationals work in South Africa on a temporary basis).

C. Legal and Regulatory Issues

2.72. An understanding of the legal and regulatory aspects of remittances is important for analyzing the use of formal and informal channels. Different channels pose different challenges to compilers, and obtaining data on transactions depends on the menu of channels used in a country and the institutional and legal environment governing remittance transactions and data compilation. In many, though not all, countries, banks and other financial institutions are required to report their international transactions (including remittances) to central banks or other national financial authorities. However, the regulatory environment and practices substantially vary across countries in treatment of entities engaged in funds transfer and the various modes of transfer used, which has significant implications on reporting and coverage of statistics on remittances. A poor legal and communication technology infrastructure may hinder the regulation of some kinds of entities in some countries, thus posing challenges for reporting, whereas in others, the entities may be regulated and supervised by a number of different agencies, creating data overlaps and challenges to compilers who need to integrate these different data sets.

2.73. Recent emphasis on regulatory issues in remittances has come from the Financial Action Task Force (FATF) on money laundering and financing of terrorism. The FATF has issued recommendations that urge countries to implement a regulatory framework by registering or licensing money or value transfer providers. An important element of the framework in some countries is encouraging entities providing remittance transfer services to identify themselves. Registration schemes have been adopted in countries with a large number of informal remittance providers, where a primary goal is to identify the institutions involved. In contrast, in licensing regimes, providers are filtered, ex ante, and must demonstrate their ability to comply with regulatory directives. In both regimes, providers must comply with certain information gathering and reporting requirements, in particular:

- Customer identification: Providers of financial services must ensure that their clients are identified (e.g., by passport or national identification card); this could be particularly problematic in the remittance sector, where customers are often undocumented or illegal migrants and short-term workers.
- Record keeping: Providers have to maintain an appropriate record of transactions and of customer identification data; the records should be made available to the authorities when needed.
- Suspicious transactions reporting: Providers must report information to the authorities on transactions that may be connected with illegal purposes.

2.74. Also common to both registration and licensing regimes is the ongoing monitoring of activities through reporting to the authorities. This aspect is obviously important from a statistical compilation perspective. Reporting may consist of periodically (e.g., annually or quarterly) submitting to authorities information on all transactions. The amount of detail provided varies from country to country, from only occasional reporting of very aggregate information (e.g., annual turnover) to full details for individual transactions, such as customer name, place of work, nationality, passport or other identification number, transferred amount, beneficiary/sender name, partner country, and purpose of transfer.

2.75. Although the FATF recommendations have increased the extent and uniformity of regulation of the remittance industry, including of the MTO sector, this industry is not homogeneously regulated across countries. This is partly due to the general nature of the recommendations themselves, which provide wide latitude to countries. Moreover, in cash-based and low-income countries, implementation and administration of an adequate regulatory framework is particularly problematic. A variety of public agencies (e.g., central banks, financial or money laundering supervisors, local authorities, and customs and tax authorities) share the responsibility to supervise MTOs and other remittance providers in some countries, whereas in other countries MTOs are largely unregulated. Depending on the regulatory framework, regulatory data may be available for statistical purposes (and data being collected for regulatory purposes can often also be adapted for statistical purposes). In some countries, regulatory information is used for statistical purposes, and in other countries independent statistical data collection activities are undertaken.

2.76. Countries often also adopt a regulatory framework, with a set of statistical regulations, directly addressing statistical activities. They define the institutions responsible for the various broad statistical areas, the type of information to be collected, the population of respondents, and their statistical obligations. Sanctions are sometimes imposed for missing or incorrect reporting. Central banks typically have the power to require banks and other financial intermediaries to report statistical information on their operations, including cross-border transactions, carried out on their own behalf or on behalf of clients. Consequently, in most countries central banks are able to conduct indirect data collections on payments (i.e., reporting the information on behalf of customers) through the information on cross-border settlement that banks undertake on behalf of MTO agents and other entities. In countries that have foreign exchange controls, recording, verification, and reporting requirements are likely to apply. However, in countries with less rigorous financial regulation and supervision, many types of entities undertaking money transfer activities may not be reporting data that are adequate or useful for statistical compilation, thus posing a challenge to remittance compilation.

2.77. Countries where central banks are at the same time balance of payments compilers and supervisors are in a better position to impose the statistical obligation to report transactions directly (i.e., not via banks used for settlements). If it does not contrast with any legal provision, another possibility would be to use the information reported for supervisory needs for statistical purposes as well.

CHAPTER

3 Concepts and Components

3.1. Remittances represent household income from foreign economies arising mainly from the temporary or permanent movement of people to those economies.[22] Remittances include cash and noncash items that flow through formal channels, such as electronic wire, or through informal channels, such as money or goods carried across borders. They largely consist of funds and noncash items sent or given by individuals who have migrated to a new economy and become residents there, and the net compensation of border, seasonal, or other short-term workers who are temporarily employed in an economy in which they are not resident.

3.2. *BPM6* identifies standard components and provides supplementary items to allow compilation of remittance aggregates. No single data item in the balance of payments framework comprehensively captures transactions in remittances. This chapter explains the different items needed to calculate remittance aggregates and the relationships between the different aggregates.

3.3. Remittances are derived mainly from two items in the balance of payments framework: income earned by workers in economies where they are not resident (or from nonresident employers) and transfers from residents of one economy to residents of another. The definitions of those items, as well as other relevant definitions and concepts, are set out below.

3.4. The following section contains a number of quotations. All of them are from *BPM6*.

[22]The definitions of standard components of the balance of payments accounts are somewhat broader than this, because they are not based on the concepts of migration, employment, or family relationships.

A. Underlying Concepts

Residence

3.5. The balance of payments framework rests on the identification of residents and nonresidents of a reporting economy. According to *BPM6*, "[t]he residence of households is determined according to the centre of predominant economic interest of its members." The general guideline for applying this principle is "being present for one year or more in a territory or intending to do so is sufficient to qualify" as being a resident of that economy. Short trips to other countries—for recreation or work—do not lead to a change of residence, but going abroad with the intention of staying one year or longer does. "If a member of an existing household ceases to reside in the territory where this household is resident, the individual ceases to be a member of that household." Persons going abroad to work thus become residents of the host country when they plan to stay for a year or longer, but they can rejoin their original household on return. In addition, there are guidelines for residence for specific cases of students, medical patients, and ship's crew as well as diplomats, military personnel, and civil servants employed abroad in government enclaves. Regardless of the length of stay in a host economy, these groups are considered residents of the originating economy.

3.6. Residence is important for remittances data because remittance transactions are recorded differently depending on the residence status of the workers in their host economy. Border, seasonal, and other short-term workers are not resident in the economy where they work, and their gross income from employment is recorded as "compensation of employees." There are no entries for the wages of migrants, because they are residents of the same economy as their employer (assuming that their employer is a resident entity). However, when they send remittances to another country, these are recorded as "personal transfers."

3.7. In many cases, it is assumed that the entities employing workers are resident in the economy where the work is performed. However, nonresident employers, which include embassies, other diplomatic missions, and international organizations, may have a substantial impact on remittances data. When resident workers work for nonresident employers, their wages and other benefits are recorded as "compensation of employees." In this circumstance, their gross income from employment will count as remittances, but these employees of nonresident employers have not migrated or traveled beyond the geographic border of their home country. Under balance of payments concepts, embassies, diplomatic missions, and international organizations are not considered to be part of the economy in which they may physically exist.

Transactions in balance of payments statistics

3.8. "Every transaction is either an exchange or a transfer. An exchange involves a provision of something of economic value in return for a counterpart item of economic value." "A transfer is a counterpart entry that offsets the provision of a nonfinancial or financial item by an entity to another entity without a counterpart return of an item of economic value." This means that transfers indicate one-sided transactions, without a quid pro quo. In the remittances context, transactions recorded as compensation of employees are exchanges and those recorded as personal transfers are transfers.

3.9. Capital transfers "result in a commensurate change in the stocks of assets of one or both parties to the transaction without affecting the savings of either party." Capital transfers in kind are transfers of ownership of nonfinancial assets or forgiveness of debt. A transfer of cash is a capital transfer only when it is linked to or conditional on the acquisition or disposal of a fixed asset. "Current transfers consist of all transfers that are not capital transfers. Current transfers directly affect the level of disposable income."

3.10. Transactions are sometimes labeled as debits or credits to indicate their direction. A debit is associated with a financial outflow (and payments of income or transfers); a credit, with a financial inflow (and receipts of income or transfers). Thus, a remittance credit entry refers to the receipt of remittances, and a remittance debit entry refers to the payment of remittances.[23]

[23]For further details on accounting principles, including the double entry principle, refer to *BPM6*.

Valuation

3.11. All valuations in the balance of payments framework are based on market values. "Market prices for transactions are defined as amounts of money that willing buyers pay to acquire something from willing sellers; the exchanges are made between independent parties and on the basis of commercial considerations only."

3.12. Compensation of employees comprises wages and salaries in cash, wages and salaries in kind, and employers' social contributions. Also included are all forms of bonuses and allowances. All transfers in kind should be valued at the market value of the goods or services provided to the recipient—that is, the current exchange value. The valuation of cash transfers is obvious, whereas transfers of other financial assets should be recorded at market value.

Timing

3.13. Compensation of employees and transfers are recorded on an accrual basis. In the case of voluntary transfers, accrual and settlement are identical. However, this is not the case with compulsory transfers (such as taxes or alimony), which should in principle be recorded when accrued, although this can be difficult in practice.

B. Standard Components

3.14. Two items in the balance of payments framework that substantially relate to remittances are "compensation of employees" and "personal transfers." Both of these standard components are recorded in the current account (see Table 3.1).

Compensation of employees

3.15. Compensation of employees refers to the income of border, seasonal, and other short-term workers who work in an economy where they are not resident, and to the income of resident workers who are employed by a nonresident entity. Compensation of employees "represents remuneration in return for the labor input to the production process contributed by an individual in an employer-employee relationship with the enterprise." Compensation of employees is recorded gross and includes amounts paid by the employee as taxes or for other purposes in the economy where the work is performed.

Table 3.1. Components Required for Compiling Remittance Items and Their Related Account and Description

Component	Related Balance of Payments Account and Description
1. Compensation of employees	Primary income account, standard component
2. Personal transfers	Secondary income account, standard component
3. Travel and transportation related to temporary employment	Goods and services account, supplementary item
4. Taxes and social contributions related to temporary employment	Secondary income account, supplementary item
5. Compensation of employees less expenses related to temporary employment	Primary income account (for compensation of employees), goods and services account (for travel and transportation expenses) and secondary income account (for taxes and social contributions), supplementary item
6. Capital transfers between households	Capital account, supplementary item
7. Social benefits	Secondary income account, supplementary item
8. Current transfers to NPISHs	Secondary income account, supplementary item
9. Capital transfers to NPISHs	Capital account, supplementary item

Note: Important relationships:
- "Net" compensation of employees (5): 1 minus the sum of 3 and 4
- Personal remittances: 2 plus 5 plus 6
- Total remittances: 2 plus 5 plus 6 plus 7
- Total remittances plus transfers to NPISHs: 2 plus 5 plus 6 plus 7 plus 8 plus 9

NPISH = nonprofit institution serving households.

Table 3.2. Tabular Presentation of Remittances Concepts in *BPM6*

<table>
<tr><td colspan="6">Total remittances and transfers to NPISHs: a+b+c+d+e+f</td></tr>
<tr><td colspan="4">Total remittances: a+b+c+d</td><td rowspan="2">e</td><td rowspan="2">f</td></tr>
<tr><td colspan="3">Personal remittances: a+b+c</td><td rowspan="2">d
Social benefits</td></tr>
<tr><td>a
Personal transfers (part of current transfers)</td><td>b
Compensation of employees less taxes, social contributions, transport, and travel</td><td>c
Capital transfers between households</td><td>Current transfers to NPISHs</td><td>Capital transfers to NPISHs</td></tr>
</table>

Source: IMF, 2008 (*BPM6*).
Note: "Personal transfers" is a standard item; other items are supplementary.

3.16. The earnings of nonresident workers who sell services to another economy but who are not employees of a nonresident company are not included in compensation of employees (see *BPM6* for the definition of an employer-employee relationship that clarifies the difference between "compensation of employees" and sales of services).

Personal transfers

3.17. "Personal transfers consist of all current transfers in cash or in kind made or received by resident households to or from nonresident households. Personal transfers thus include all current transfers between resident and nonresident individuals." Therefore, personal transfers are a subset of current transfers. They cover all current transfers that are sent by individuals to individuals.[24]

[24]"Personal transfers" replaces an item known as "workers' remittances" in *BPM5*. However, workers' remittances are included as a supplementary item in *BPM6*. Unlike workers' remittances, which are defined as current transfers made by employees to residents of another economy, personal transfers are defined independently of the source of income of the sending household, the relationship between the households, and the purpose for which the transfer is made. Simplifying the definition brought it in line with compilation practices applied in many countries (which did not take account of factors such as source of income and purpose).

3.18. Although remittances are related to migration and the sender and receiver often are relatives living in different countries, this is not explicitly part of the definition. Nonetheless, it is recognized that personal transfers often originate from migrants sending resources to support their relatives in their country of origin.

C. Supplementary Items

3.19. There are three major supplementary items related to remittances: personal remittances, total remittances, and total remittances and transfers to nonprofit institutions serving households (NPISHs). They are cumulative measures, as illustrated in Table 3.2. As supplementary items, their compilation and dissemination are encouraged but voluntary depending on the needs of the compiling economy.

Personal remittances

3.20. Personal remittances are defined as current and capital transfers in cash or in kind between resident households and nonresident households, plus net compensation of employees. In short, personal remittances include all household-to-household transfers and the net compensation of nonresident workers.

3.21. Compensation of employees includes gross earnings of nonresident workers. Net compensation is calculated by deducting taxes, social contributions paid by nonresident workers in the country of employment, and transport and travel expenditures related to their work abroad from (gross) compensation.

- "Taxes" deducted from the compensation of employees are current taxes on income that consist of taxes payable by short-term workers to the host country's government on income earned from the provision of labor. Taxes on wages and salaries earned by nonresident employees are recorded as payable by nonresident employees and are included in gross compensation of employees.
- "Social contributions" are the actual or imputed contributions made by households to social insurance schemes to make provision for social benefits to be paid. Social insurance schemes include social security schemes (which cover the entire community or large sections of it and are imposed, controlled, and financed by government) and employment-related schemes (including funded and unfunded pension schemes).
- "Transport" is the process of carriage of people and objects from one location to another as well as related supporting and auxiliary services. International transport services are included in this item, and local transport expenditures of nonresident workers in the host country are attributed to "travel."
- "Travel" refers to the acquisition of goods and services in an economy by individuals who are visiting and not resident in that economy. It also includes acquisitions of goods and services by border, seasonal, and short-term cross-border workers in their economy of employment.[25] In practice, it may be difficult to separate travel related to temporary employment from all other travel.[26]

Total remittances

3.22. Total remittances is the sum of "personal remittances" and social benefits. "Social benefits include benefits payable under social security funds and pension funds. They may be in cash or in kind." This item includes all household income obtained from working abroad. Total remittances includes income from individuals working abroad for short periods, income from individuals residing abroad, and social benefits from abroad.

Total remittances and transfers to nonprofit institutions serving households

3.23. This item includes "total remittances" and both current and capital transfers to NPISHs from any sector of the sending economy. It therefore includes all transfers benefiting households directly or indirectly through NPISHs, as well as the net earnings of short-term workers abroad. It even includes donations, in cash or in kind, from governments and enterprises to charitable organizations in another economy. It therefore is a very wide definition that is not closely linked to migration. In fact, much private and official aid as well as cross-border sponsorship of educational

[25] In *BPM6*, travel excludes the acquisition of valuables, consumer durables, and other consumer purchases that are included in general merchandise.

[26] Estimates can be used to approximate employment-related travel (see Chapter 5). Supplementary items on acquisition of goods and services, including transport, by border, seasonal, and other short-term workers, were introduced within the transport and travel standard items in *BPM6*.

Box 3.1. Comparison of Measures of Personal Remittances in *BPM5* and *BPM6* Frameworks

A. *BPM5* Framework (Standard components related to remittances)

Income—Compensation of employees
Receivable (Credit)
Payable (Debit)

Current transfers—Other sectors
Workers' remittances
Receivable (Credit)
Payable (Debit)

Capital account—Migrant transfers
Receivable (Credit)
Payable (Debit)

B. *BPM6* Framework (Components related to remittances)

***Income—Compensation of employees* (standard component)**
Receivable (Credit)
Payable (Debit)

***Personal remittances* (supplementary item)**
Receivable (Credit)
Net compensation of employees
*Compensation of employees (*standard component*)*
Less (expenses abroad of cross-border workers):
Taxes on income (paid to nonresidents)
Social contributions (paid to nonresidents)
International transport (import)
Travel (import)
Personal transfers (standard component)
Workers' remittances
Other household-to-household transfers

Personal remittances
Payable (Debit)
Net Compensation of employees
*Compensation of employees (*standard component*)*
Less (expenses in the compiling economy of cross-border workers):
Taxes on income (received from nonresidents)
Social contributions (received from nonresidents)
International transport (export)
Travel (export)
Personal transfers (standard component)
Workers' remittances
Other household-to-household transfers

Note: Based on contributions from the Central Bank of Russia.

and cultural activities (including scholarships) may be included in this item.[27]

3.24. The identification of NPISHs is not without challenges. Whereas NPISHs are part of the wider household sector, nonprofit institutions serving other sectors are not. Compilers generally will be able to appropriately identify the NPISHs resident in their economy, but they may find it more problematic to identify NPISHs in partner economies. This may make the compilation of debit transactions of "total remittances and transfers to NPISHs" challenging because the definition is partially based on identifying the sector of the transacting party in the partner economy.

[27]Of the new supplementary remittance aggregates in the international accounts, some data users consider "total remittances and transfers to nonprofit institutions serving households" to most closely match the economic concept of remittances (see Section A). This measure is broader than the other remittance aggregates, because it includes current and capital transfers to NPISHs from any sector of the sending economy (households, corporations, governments, and nonprofit institutions). Thus, unlike the other supplementary remittance aggregates, it includes funds and noncash items that flow indirectly to households through nonprofit institutions.

3.25. A comparison of remittances measures in the *BPM5* and *BPM6* frameworks is presented in Box 3.1.

D. Related Concepts

Investment by migrants

3.26. Migrants frequently invest in their country of origin, whether they intend to eventually return or have left permanently. Sometimes the attachment to their country of origin, and the willingness to invest there, carries over to subsequent generations. Such investments can take numerous forms, but financial investments (notably bank deposits and portfolio investments) and investments in real estate are probably most common. Small enterprises, located in the country of origin and sometimes managed by relatives, can also benefit from investments by migrants.

3.27. Cross-border investments such as those mentioned in the preceding paragraph are recorded in the financial account. Although investment flows from migrants are of analytical interest in the context of the economic effects of migration, they are not remittances. The qualitative analysis of investment flows is needed to identify the effects of migration on investment patterns. Analyzing the motives of migrant investors in choosing assets in their country of origin over other assets would be relevant for policymaking purposes, but is beyond the scope of this compilation guide.

3.28. However, in some cases investment transactions by migrants may be vehicles for the provision of remittances, notably when relatives enjoy access to resources or benefit from the use of fixed assets. When migrants deposit funds in their accounts in their country of origin and relatives have access to these funds, their withdrawals are personal transfers. For joint accounts, as a statistical convention, a transfer can be recorded when the funds move across borders rather than when they are withdrawn. When a migrant purchases real estate and relatives occupy it without paying market rents, or when a migrant establishes an enterprise and relatives are employed and paid above-market wages by this enterprise, personal transfers can be imputed. In the individual case, transfer values would be calculated as the difference between actual transactions and market-equivalent values. In practice, it is difficult to identify such transfers and calculate their value. If larger patterns are known to compilers—if, for example, there are large numbers of migrants buying real estate for use by their relatives in the home country—estimates can be made on the basis of aggregate transactions data and benchmarks.

Returning migrants

3.29. While migrants reside in a host economy, their remittances will be recorded as current or capital transfers. These include gifts in cash and in kind to their household of origin. When returning home, many migrants bring goods or own assets that will, on return, be owned by their household of origin. However, cash, consumer durables and other goods, and other assets that migrants own on return to their home country are not recorded as transfers. In addition, goods that migrants bring with them on return are not the subject of balance of payments transactions and therefore are excluded from balance of payments transactions.[28] Assets (such as bank balances and real estate ownership) are recorded as a reclassification in the international investment position because the residence of the owner changes but no change of ownership takes place.

3.30. Although the distinction between a transaction and a reclassification of residence is important for the structure of the international accounting system, the effect of remittance sending and returning migrants on households and countries is much the same. Data users who are interested in understanding all contributions that migrants may make to their households and economies of origin should note this and may wish to make additional estimations.

Resident-to-resident transactions across borders

3.31. Other transactions that can easily be mistaken for remittances are payments made by individuals to individuals when both parties are resident in the same economy but one party is temporarily present in another economy. Nonresident workers, such as diplomats, military personnel, and other civil servants employed abroad in government enclaves, sending money from the economy in which enclaves are located to relatives in their country of residence are performing a resident-to-resident transfer that (as such) is not recorded as a balance of payments transaction. Balance of payments transfers do not include transfers to a household member by another household member who is temporarily in another country, such as families supporting relatives who are students or medical patients abroad. Although these transfers involve residents of the same country and are therefore not included in balance of payments statistics, related transactions (e.g., financial flows through banks, related service charges, travel expenses payable to nonresident entities, and compensation of employees) may be included.

Bilateral data

3.32. Although data on remittance flows between major partner countries are often provided on a supplementary basis in balance of payments data, such detailed geographic data are not a standard component of the accounts. Data users have usually empha-

[28]In *BPM5*, the net worth of persons changing their residence was recorded in "migrants' transfers" in the capital account. In *BPM6*, this amount is recorded in "other changes in volume" and not in transactions.

Box 3.2. Personal Remittances and GATS Presence of Natural Persons

GATS defines four modes of supply. In addition to the cross-border supply (mode 1), where both the supplier and the consumer remain in their respective home territories, GATS also covers cases where consumers are present outside their home territory to consume services (mode 2), or cases where service suppliers are present in the territory of the consumers to provide their services, whether by establishing a commercial presence (mode 3), or through the presence of natural persons (mode 4). Mode 4 occurs when an individual (at whatever skill level) has moved temporarily into the territory of the consumer to provide a service. Mode 4 is generally understood as covering:

- *Contractual services suppliers*, whether *employees of the foreign service supplier* or *self-employed*. These persons enter the country of the consumer in the context of a service contract;
- *Intra-corporate transferees*. The service supplier has commercial presence abroad and sends its employee to its affiliate. The supply of service to the consumer is carried out through a commercial presence;[1] and
- *Service sellers/persons responsible for setting up commercial presence*. There is initially no actual service supply for this category of persons.[2]

According to the above description, to measure mode 4 trade flows (i.e., the contractual service supply) it is necessary to identify (or estimate) the relevant part in balance of payments services transactions considered as mode 4 supply.[3]

While personal remittances provide information on a country's income generated through persons temporarily moving abroad or migrating, personal remittances do not equate with mode 4 trade flows, as described above. Important differences exist in terms of coverage of persons. For example, personal remittances may cover earnings related to employment in non-services sectors as well as earnings of persons employed by international organizations.

[1]The mode 4 commitment guarantees the right of the person to be present, to enable the service supplier to supply a service through its affiliate.

[2]Their movement in order to conduct negotiations is guaranteed by commitments under mode 4.

[3]However, this may be difficult, because a single international transaction in services may include several modes of supply.

sized accurate reporting of aggregate remittance flows as a higher priority than geographic detail, but requests for bilateral data are nonetheless made regularly. The compilation and reporting of bilateral flows is therefore encouraged, especially for major remittances corridors. Bilateral data are discussed further in Chapter 5.

Supply of services by natural persons

3.33. Personal remittances do not substitute for indicators for measuring trade flows (mode 4) under the General Agreement on Trade in Services (GATS). The difference between remittances statistics and GATS mode 4 statistics is presented in Box 3.2.

CHAPTER

4 Data Sources and Estimation Methods

4.1. Difficulty in obtaining more accurate source data is the biggest obstacle to improving data on remittances. Any strategy for improving remittances data should, therefore, review current data sources, assess possible other data sources, and develop a data improvement strategy based on data needs and priorities as well as resource constraints.

4.2. The quality of statistical data is often measured primarily by their accuracy, coverage, timeliness, and frequency. Other aspects that compilers have to consider in choosing data sources are their costs and other practical obstacles, such as legal and institutional factors.

4.3. This chapter outlines options for developing a data collection program for remittances data by discussing the main approaches to obtaining data. These are an international transactions reporting system (ITRS), direct reporting by remittance service providers, household surveys, and the use of secondary source data, such as demographic, administrative, and macroeconomic data. The final section provides a tabular comparison of these data sources.

A. International Transactions Reporting Systems

4.4. Unlike many data sources that compilers may have to develop for the purpose of improving remittances data, an ITRS is part of the broader institutional data collection framework of many countries. Where an ITRS exists and produces useful data, compilers are encouraged to evaluate its usefulness in estimating remittances. This section discusses the use of an ITRS in compiling data on remittances and also outlines features of an ITRS, what data can be obtained, and how to address data weaknesses. In countries that do not have an ITRS, this data source is not a current option.[29]

Description of the collection system

4.5. An ITRS is a data collection system that obtains data from banks and enterprises at the level of individual transactions. ITRSs vary from fully comprehensive closed systems to open systems. A fully comprehensive closed ITRS collects data on all resident–nonresident transactions and reconciles them with corresponding changes in asset or liability positions. It must therefore include both cash transactions (which are reconciled with resident banks' foreign currency positions) and noncash transactions (which are reconciled with other assets and liabilities with nonresidents). Open ITRSs are often partially comprehensive, insofar as they do not register all transactions and do not match flows and changes in positions. In this case, additional source data may be needed to reconcile flows with changes in positions.

4.6. Under both open and closed ITRSs, data are generally collected on a mandatory basis from domestic banks and other relevant entities that hold foreign assets or operate in the foreign currency market. These banks and entities are required to file regular reports on all transactions channeled through the foreign exchange payment system, as well as on assets and liabilities with nonresidents. To achieve a good level of coverage, an ITRS should identify virtually all resident units engaged in transactions with nonresidents, and obtain relevant data from them. With a few exceptions, they stem from systems originally designed to monitor and control foreign exchange transactions.[30] In some cases, foreign exchange control systems evolved into ITRSs after exchange restrictions were lifted. However, in many cases ITRSs are still strongly linked to control and supervision, with both positive and negative impacts on balance of payments compilation.

4.7. In regard to positive impacts on compilation, ITRSs linked to control and supervision systems are

[29]The *RCG* does not propose that an ITRS be implemented for the sole purpose of compiling remittances data.

[30]In some countries, ITRSs were developed independently from an exchange control system.

less likely to experience problems related to timeliness and noncompliance with reporting requirements because control and supervision usually rely on strong legislation. In addition, such ITRSs do not represent a substantial additional burden in themselves, because data reporting is not an end but instead a by-product of the foreign exchange monitoring and control framework. In regard to negative impacts, when control or supervision are the main purposes of a system, providing data for balance of payments compilation may not be regarded as a core function of the system, and the ITRS data therefore may be less reliable (because statistical needs may be de-emphasized in programs with primarily regulatory or administrative purposes).

ITRS and data on remittances

4.8. Remittance transactions are frequently carried out through the international payments system. In countries with both foreign exchange controls and an ITRS, this means that the transactions are routed through the banking system (or other institutions with foreign exchange licenses and subject to data reporting requirements) and therefore registered in the ITRS. For this reason, the ITRS is often seen by balance of payments compilers as an important and efficient source of information. Provided that the ITRS is reliable, compilers focus on the records of the intermediary banks that carry out the cross-border payments on behalf of other remittance service providers (e.g., MTOs and credit unions) or on their own behalf in order to obtain remittances data.

Remittances captured by the ITRS by transaction channels

4.9. By design, an ITRS can cover only transactions reported by participating institutions through which funds are transferred using international settlement systems. Typically, reporters are commercial banks and other licensed foreign exchange transactors. In many economies, a significant volume of remittances is channeled through international payments systems because banks and other financial institutions settle their payments formally, either on their own behalf or as a service provider for third parties. Where banks and other financial institutions offer remittance services at competitive rates and from convenient locations, and where the regulatory burden for sending and receiving remittances is not high, banking channels have gained importance.[31]

4.10. Given that the MTOs use banks for cross-border payments, an ITRS is, in principle, able to capture international flows between and within MTO networks. Nevertheless, a separation between settlement arrangements and information flow, as well as the involvement of clearing centers and netting between regional MTOs, may result in the omission of larger gross flows. These factors also make it difficult for reporting banks to fully identify personal transfers or provide an adequate breakdown by country.[32]

4.11. An ITRS may be an effective data collection tool for transactions by credit unions. When credit unions provide remittance services themselves and transfer funds via international payment systems, the transactions can be measured using the ITRS.

4.12. The situation could be different in the case of postal networks. In some countries, national postal services may not fall under the legal authority of financial and statistical authorities and therefore may not be subject to data reporting obligations. Under such circumstances, an ITRS is not an efficient source for the collection of remittances through the postal system. Nonetheless, the ITRS may sometimes be used as a starting point to assess the importance of this transfer channel. The reason is that national post offices normally settle their mutual claims periodically using the international banking system. In countries where privately owned postal banks are subject to the same legal requirements as other banks, their activities can be captured through the ITRS.

4.13. The ITRS would not cover remittances via courier companies, through which cash is delivered physically. In some parts of the world, remittances are transferred through cellular phone charge cards, stored value cards, and also through some newer forms of remittances using cellular phones An ITRS will in most cases not be able to identify and obtain data on those transactions because the companies involved in the transactions—such as telecommunications firms or

[31]If the originating bank and its partner bank in the receiving country act as the service provider when a cash transfer is made, relevant information about the sender and the final recipient may be available to separate the remittance transactions from other business transactions. This is less frequently the case when other agents, such as MTOs, are the point of contact with clients. In any case, banks may find it challenging to distinguish personal transfers from other current transfers.

[32]MTOs separate the information flow and financial settlement related to a transaction. Therefore, MTOs can provide very fast remittance services by communicating (e.g., through the Internet) transactions between distant branches. Settlements for numerous transactions can then be batched to a single cross-border net payment.

Table 4.1. Coverage of Remittance Aggregates Through an ITRS

Remittance Aggregate	Data Generally Obtainable from an ITRS
Personal transfers	Current transfers through ITRS reporters (i.e., banks and other financial institutions); net settlements of other formal channels (e.g., money transfer operators); no information on transactions through other channels or transfers in kind
Personal remittances	Current and capital transfers through ITRS reporters; coverage of compensation of employees or expenditure related to short-term work abroad (travel, taxes, etc.) only in exceptional cases (when payments are made though reporting banks and nonresident workers are identified)
Total remittances	Current and capital transfers to households, including social benefits and transfer from NPISHs
Total remittances and transfers to NPISHs	Current and capital transfers to households, including social benefits and transfer from NPISHs, as well as current and capital transfers to NPISHs

Note: ITRS = international transactions reporting system. Transactions are captured only if they are made through institutions that are ITRS reporters; some items may not be readily identifiable although they are included (e.g., current transfers to NPISHs are included but not separately identifiable in current transfers).

retailers—may not operate their internal data systems to detect balance of payments transactions, and are typically not subject to reporting of third-party transactions. Remittances through such channels as hawala, remittances in kind, and cash transported by individuals will also not be captured by the ITRS.

Remittances captured by an ITRS by type of transaction

4.14. Data obtained from an ITRS cover cross-border transactions settled by banks and other financial intermediaries. With a few exceptions, they do not cover transactions by residents and nonresidents settled domestically, especially when no exchange of currency takes place (see Table 4.1). Therefore, an ITRS does not fully cover compensation of employees, nor does it detect what nonresident workers spend on travel or pay in taxes in their host country. At the same time, an ITRS may include data that should not be included in remittances, such as money sent by a nonresident worker from the host economy to a household in the home economy.

4.15. Given the right legal and institutional circumstances, an ITRS may be an effective tool for obtaining data on personal transfers, capital transfers between households (if the identification of households is possible), and current and capital transfers to NPISHs (if the identification of NPISHs is possible).[33] It may also enable compilers to identify social contributions and benefits.

4.16. Depending on the design of an ITRS, it may be difficult for reporting institutions to distinguish household-to-household transfers from transactions between households and other sectors. With account-to-account transfers, the institutions may have sufficient information to classify clients in the reporting economy according to sector, but the necessary information may seldom be available for the nonresident counterpart to the transaction.[34] In regard to classifying clients in the reporting economy by sector, in many countries the residence status of clients must be provided, because transactions with nonresident accounts are treated differently from transactions between resident accounts for reasons such as legal requirements, anti–money laundering measures, or different fee structures.

4.17. If banks report for clients like MTOs, the sector information and residence status for all individual transactions that relate to a single settlement payment may not be available to the reporting bank (and would need to be requested from the client). Although the reporter could request information about individual clients from the MTO, this could significantly increase reporting burden (and may not result in accurate information).

[33]However, the output of an ITRS typically does not allow for the breakdown between personal transfers and capital transfers without further information.

[34]In most cases, an ITRS is not able to provide information about the nonresident account holder. For this reason, misclassifications may occur regarding deposits to own accounts abroad, which represent a financial investment, and transfers to other accounts, which may constitute personal transfers.

4.18. Accurately identifying the sector and resident status of transactors is challenging for an ITRS. Without confidence that the residence of transactors can be adequately determined, personal transfers and related supplementary items (personal remittances, total remittances, and total remittances and transfers to NPISHs) cannot be compiled accurately. Furthermore, accurate classification of remittance flows also requires the identification of the sector of even the foreign transaction party. Although this may be a surmountable problem in the case of personal transfers (compilers may find indicators for identifying household-to-household transfers), it may be more difficult to solve for supplementary items (particularly total remittances, and total remittances and transfers to NPISHs) because the originating transactor can be from any sector. Information obtained directly from the transactors may facilitate more accurate classification.

Preconditions for an effective ITRS

4.19. In the absence of an appropriate legal framework that ensures that foreign transactions are channeled through licensed intermediaries and that those intermediaries report transactions data in an accurate and timely manner, incomplete coverage and delayed reporting will lead to low-quality data. It is therefore important that an ITRS be based on a legal framework that supports transactions reporting requirements appropriate to the needs of balance of payments compilation.

4.20. Regarding the ITRS implementation, some data items ideally should be collected in order to ensure the quality of the data. The items that should be included in the reporting system are a reference number for the transaction, the reference period, the identity of the transactors, the identity of the bank accepting the information from the client, the direction of the transaction, the currency used, the transaction value, the classification of the purpose of the transaction, and the country of the nonresident party.

4.21. Some ITRS frameworks allow smaller transactions to be reported in an aggregated fashion, and only larger transactions above a certain threshold are reported individually. Aggregate reporting results in the loss of information and can make the detection of errors more difficult. Remittance transactions are usually small, and it may be difficult to set reporting thresholds at a level that is appropriate for using an ITRS for compiling remittances data.

4.22. It may be most efficient if ITRS data were submitted electronically to balance of payments compiling institutions—for example, through secure Internet access or through specific electronic transmission systems. Data can be submitted in many forms, such as spreadsheets, in simpler systems, or using specific software or online databases in more complex systems. The systems should include coding schemes that require reporters to submit data classified according to predefined codes. Data quality analysis procedures, such as automatic consistency checks for codes and for missing and negative figures, for example, may be important in these systems. Data that fail certain basic consistency checks could be automatically rejected and have to be reviewed and corrected by the reporter. Other checks may include the identification of outliers and overall economic consistency of the reported data.

4.23. Electronic reporting facilitates the reporting of individual transactions by an ITRS. Reporting of individual transactions leads to a large data volume and places demands on compilers and their data systems for collecting, checking, and processing the data. Without a sound information technology infrastructure and the use of electronic forms, the costs could be prohibitive. Furthermore, higher levels of automation may help reduce the errors stemming from entry and processing. Manual (or paper-based) reporting systems reduce many of the benefits usually associated with an ITRS—namely, timely data provision at reasonable cost.

4.24. Contact between compilers and data providers is very important in a quality ITRS. This interaction facilitates correct classification of transactions and keeps compilers updated on alterations in operational procedures that can require changes in the data collection system in order to avoid loss of quality and coverage. The classification of transactions is done by reporting entities and, for smaller transactions, is often handled by the bank tellers with input from clients. Misclassification at this stage is one of the most important sources of errors because neither the bank staff nor clients may be familiar with balance of payments definitions.

4.25. For countries that do not have an ITRS, developing a new ITRS is costly. When exploring this option, consideration should be given to collecting more than remittances data alone. An ITRS and the related regulations (reporting requirements and foreign exchange restrictions) carry developmental, operating, and compliance costs (some borne by compiling institutions, some by reporting banks and their clients) that should be carefully evaluated.

Strengths of an ITRS as a data source

4.26. An ITRS may present significant advantages as the basic system for the compilation of remittances.

Timeliness and periodicity

4.27. An important advantage of the ITRS is its capability to deliver information to compilers in a timely and frequent manner, because data are generally registered at the moment of settlement of the transactions. The use of electronic means for collecting information by the reporting agents (banks and other financial institutions) and for transmitting reports to compilers is a precondition for maintaining high levels of timeliness and frequency.

Cost-effectiveness

4.28. In countries that have an ITRS and the appropriate regulatory and institutional framework, including foreign exchange restrictions and well-defined data reporting frameworks, data may essentially be a by-product of exchange controls. In these circumstances, an ITRS is likely to be a cost-effective source of remittances data, even when these controls are lifted. In this case, coverage may slowly erode and alternative data sources may have to be developed.

Data accuracy and accessibility

4.29. A well-structured, comprehensive ITRS tends to measure transactions accurately. In addition, an ITRS without reporting thresholds is, in general, very useful for the compilation of transactions of small amounts such as personal transfers. However, accuracy can be limited by omissions and misclassifications, as discussed below.

4.30. In economies with an ITRS, compilers frequently have useful access to the underlying reported data, which allows for closer data checking and easier follow-up to reporting institutions. This derives from the fact that financial institutions are subject to supervision by central banks who, in turn, tend to have authority to oversee the ITRS and to compile balance of payments estimates.

Weaknesses of an ITRS as a data source

4.31. Compilers should be aware of some general problems that are associated with an ITRS as a data source for remittances. These problems and some possible solutions are described here.

Omissions

4.32. In many instances, household-to-household transactions are conducted primarily through informal channels. In this case, an ITRS, which relies exclusively on remittances sent through formal channels, may present significant omissions, especially in personal transfers. When there are large informal transactions and hence transactions for which neither stock positions nor flows are reported, the ITRS cannot overcome the omissions, whether it is open or closed. In addition, there are cases where even flows through formal channels are only captured partially. This can result from netted settlements of flows through the international payments system. It is important that compilers be familiar with the structure of the remittance market in their economies in order to identify flows that bypass an ITRS and to design appropriate complementary or alternative data sources.

Misclassification

4.33. Misclassifications are a frequently identified problem with ITRS-based compilation systems because intermediaries are responsible for classifying transactions. Small transactions are especially often classified as "transfers," although they may be payments for goods or services or constitute investments (e.g., savings by residents or nonresidents). Further, it cannot always be assumed that funds transferred through MTOs are exclusively remittances. For instance, transfers to family members studying abroad or transfers to travelers undertaking lengthy trips are frequently made using payment transfer service providers. Because these person-to-person payments are also in small amounts, it may be impossible to distinguish them, in practice, from remittance flows or own personal transfers for intermediary banks or the service providers. Compilers should therefore make appropriate corrections based on benchmark data and other indicators.

Loss of information owing to reporting thresholds

4.34. An important aspect in the context of international remittances and other household-to-household payments is the fact that the average value of these payments is relatively small compared to the value of other transactions collected in the balance of payments. The low value is problematic insofar as it is not unusual that countries that use an ITRS to collect balance of payments data (in total or in part) have implemented reporting thresholds in order to reduce reporting costs and reduce the data compilation burden. The reporting threshold is a major issue regarding comprehensiveness for the compilation of remittances data.

4.35. There are two types of reporting thresholds—exemption and simplification—that are usually established to limit the statistical burden for the respondents as much as possible.

4.36. Under exemption thresholds, reporters do not have to report the transactions that fall below a predetermined amount. Because these thresholds are often fixed at a value that ensures that a substantial amount of commercial transactions are also exempted, compilers have to face the fact that a significant percentage of remittances may fall below the threshold and cannot be captured by the collection system.[35]

4.37. Simplification thresholds allow for the reporting of data in batches or in net values, in many cases without the obligation to disclose information that is relevant to the compilation of personal transfers, such as the purpose of the transaction, average amount of remittances, country of origin of remittances, and names of senders or beneficiaries.[36] The absence of certain basic information leads to distortions and limitations of the quality of remittances statistics compiled with the use of ITRS data.

4.38. One means of overcoming the problems is to rule that certain types of transactions that fall below the threshold be reported collectively (to replace the exemption by the simplification threshold) and properly identified. In this case, all lower-value transactions classified as personal transfers would be reported.

4.39. Another solution may be to contact the most relevant banks that are known to be active in the remittances business and request that they report all transactions below the threshold that they could identify as remittances. In principle, such a distinction from business transactions is possible if banks, whether acting as agents on behalf of an MTO or as service providers themselves, have the necessary details about the sender and receiver (private persons).

4.40. As long as compilers analyze the national remittances market with a focus on major service providers and impose on them only additional information requests, substantial underreporting can be avoided without leaving the "ITRS path." However, if such a solution cannot be realized, the existence of an exemption threshold may imply the need to resort to a complementary if not alternative data collection system.

Settlements of net amounts

4.41. MTOs, postal savings banks, credit card companies, and some other remittance service providers operating with well-known partners around the globe typically offset their transfers to their partners against the funds they receive from them in order to keep payments as small as possible and thus reduce costs. Multilateral networks also offset third-country claims and liabilities, settling one net position from a central settlement location. Therefore, only the net amounts—not the gross flows needed for the compilation of statistics—are reported. This is particularly problematic for countries that record both significant inflows and outflows of personal transfers.

4.42. A slightly different situation, which resembles the netting issue, arises in the case in which global service providers internalize the cross-border part of the transfer—in other words, running compensating accounts in both the sending and the receiving country. Under these arrangements, the sender in one country credits a domestic account of the MTO or bank, and the receiver in another country is paid out from a domestic account (which is an account of a partner company of the MTO or bank) in that country. The transfer itself is recorded only in the books of the company, and the ITRS system normally cannot capture these internalized transfers.

4.43. However, because compilers can assume that at some point the service provider must transfer funds to stock up the account in the receiving country, the transaction will then be reported within the framework of the ITRS. As long as the time lag between the initial transfer by the sender and the internal compensatory payment by the service provider is not too long, and as long as there are not seasonal patterns to the settlements, the ITRS may still be able to provide the relevant data with acceptable quality. It would become

[35]In the European Union, cross-border settlements below €12,500 are exempted from reporting obligations. Moreover, the European Commission proposed a new draft regulation asking to increase the reporting threshold up to €50,000 by January 2010 and to complete exemption of payment service providers for balance of payments reporting by January 2012. The draft regulation has been proposed to the European Parliament and Council.

[36]Batching of data is relevant not only in the context of simplification thresholds, but also when the information flow is separated from the funds flow, which is not rare in the remittances business. In this case, providers of remittance services may intend to batch the small amounts of the individual transfers into a single payment.

problematic if such payments were to take place, for example, only on a quarterly or biannual basis. Under such circumstances, it would also be likely that the compensation would no longer be classified by the reporter as an (aggregated) remittance transfer but, instead, as a financial or service transaction between affiliated enterprises. Such a misclassification and the time lag could lead to distortions in remittances flows statistics of the compiling country.

4.44. As in other cases in which the ITRS functions as an indirect data source, in order to avoid underreporting, timing problems, or misclassification in such cases, compilers should contact major service providers in their economy to assess the relevance of this problem and to establish specific reporting requirements if necessary.

Lack of bilateral data

4.45. It is possible to encounter difficulties in obtaining reliable data on partner countries when using an ITRS because settlements are often made through third countries. Overseas clearing centers account for a large share of settlements made by MTOs.

4.46. This shortcoming of the ITRS could be solved by approaching the major MTOs for data with a country breakdown according to the final receivers of the funds. Although this information is available to MTOs, extracting and providing it will pose an extra reporting burden and may result in MTOs rejecting information requests from compilers. Under such circumstances, compilers may consider it best to focus on the most significant flows stated in the ITRS and resort to estimations for less relevant figures based on other available sources.

B. Direct Reporting by Money Transfer Operators

4.47. Direct reporting refers to the practice of obtaining data from a group of transactors directly instead of indirectly from settlement facilities. In the case of remittances, direct reporting has further advantages compared with compilation based on an ITRS alone. These include better information on gross flows (outbound and inward) and on the geographical distribution of counterparts, and greater detail and accuracy of the data collected, because the information is directly provided by the information holders, without any intermediate communication step. Also, direct reporting, considered as the collection approach based on reports of entities directly involved in remittance transactions, has been shown to be a tool to improve the quality of statistics in a cost-effective way.

4.48. This section discusses direct reporting by MTOs as a data source for the compilation of statistics on remittances. It also provides general guidelines for the design and implementation of such reporting systems. Section A discussed how an ITRS can obtain data on the settlements of MTOs; hence, the transactions of MTOs are indirectly reported by banks involved in the settlements. An ITRS captures only settlement data and therefore has incomplete coverage, and data obtained from direct reporting by MTOs can, in principle, cover all transactions channeled through MTOs (and be used to augment data obtained from an ITRS) but, by definition, will not include transactions through other channels.

Description of the collection system

4.49. Direct reporting by MTOs can be an effective data source if MTOs account for a large share of remittance transactions in the reporting economy and if an appropriate legal environment can be established to ensure that reporting requirements can be established and enforced. In many countries, MTOs play a dominant role in the remittance industry, and direct reporting seems particularly appropriate to obtaining data from them. Because transactions by banks are often covered by an ITRS, direct reporting is also a useful supplement to an ITRS, because it addresses some common weaknesses of an ITRS relating to aggregated and netted settlement payments. It is important to note, however, that a direct reporting system could be implemented not only for MTOs but also for any type of remittance service provider (Box 4.1).[37]

4.50. MTOs handle complex payments flows with numerous partner countries, resulting in complex mul-

[37]In some countries, direct reporting replaced a traditional ITRS, which relies on the monitoring of cross-border settlements, as the main collection strategy. This evolution stems from the recognition of the loss of accuracy of ITRS information because of the introduction of innovative techniques of liquidity management, especially among large companies. In an effort to reduce settlement costs, these companies increasingly adopt procedures of centralized clearing and netting of multilateral flows (e.g., cash pooling). In many countries, raising exemption thresholds for bank reporting further contributes to the need to lessen the dependence of balance of payments compilers on banks and, consequently, a more central role is assigned to reporting by nonbank institutions. For information about direct reporting methodologies in balance of payments in the European context, see Eurostat (2003).

Box 4.1. Direct Reporting by Different Remittance Service Providers

Direct reporting by MTOs is particularly useful because it overcomes the problem that data on MTOs reported in an ITRS normally reflect netted settlements rather than gross underlying transactions. Direct reporting can be set up specifically for the purpose of compiling data on remittances and can focus on the transaction-by-transaction information flow between participating MTOs.

Direct reporting can, in principle, also be applied to entities other than MTOs. For example, direct reporting by other remittance service providers such as banks and post offices could be useful even if MTOs account for a relatively large share of total transactions. Direct reporting of transfer receipts by NPISHs would help to estimate "total remittances and transfers to NPISHs." However, the transactions of NPISHs, banks, and other entities are typically covered by existing data sources such as an ITRS or surveys.

Also, informal institutions, such as those involved with hawala, could in principle report on their transactions. In practice, direct reporters are more likely to be formal entities because reporting obligations (and the definition of the reporting population) are more easily established and enforced with legal entities.

tilateral operations with an extensive use of netting of payments. Direct reporting is a promising approach for compilation of remittances data because it can take advantage of the information flow between the national centers of the international MTO network. MTOs exchange information about each transaction; the information flow is therefore more extensive and detailed than the financial flow resulting from settlement transactions. In addition, MTO data can provide useful information to be used in combination with other data sources to estimate remittance-related transactions.

Design and implementation of the collection approach

4.51. MTOs carry out a large volume of household-to-household transfers. This section discusses how a system of direct reporting can be designed and implemented to obtain data on the transactions through MTOs. It should be noted, however, that it is challenging to properly record remittance transactions through MTOs and that this data source will not capture the whole universe of such transactions.

4.52. As a start, compilers have to identify the target population for the direct reporting system on the basis of coverage and expediency. MTOs are usually franchise operations with numerous agents and subagents in each country. Agents are direct franchisees or subsidiaries of an international MTO company, whereas subagents are subordinate to a national agent. Subagents provide the branch network through which extensive services are delivered. In principle, each subagent or MTO branch could be required to report transactions data. However, it appears more effective to prefer agents as the statistical units, because they are smaller in number and can report equivalent information, because the administrative process requires agents to know all relevant details about customers and transactions.

4.53. Next, compilers have to determine the nature of the data collection because both census and sample surveys are possible. The number of agents operating in each country is often relatively small, typically ranging from 10 to a few hundred. It seems therefore feasible to conduct a census survey. However, when national circumstances require it, such as because of cost constraints, a sample survey can be considered. In this case, if a strong concentration of the market shares exists, it should be ensured that all of the largest MTOs by market share are included in the sample.

4.54. With both a census and a sample survey, a first step in collecting data from MTOs is to build a list to identify all elements of the target population (in sample approaches the list is named "sample frame"). The list is readily available in countries where the regulatory framework requires the registration or licensing of MTOs with monetary or other financial authorities. In countries where MTOs are registered only as companies, but not as financial entities, the identification of the target population may require a search of the company registry. However, all major MTOs tend to be well known and are easily identified.

4.55. Then, compilers have to decide the frequency of data collection based on data needs and practical constraints. The decision on the frequency of the data collection is country specific. Data needs depend on, among other things, the importance of remittances for the compiling economies and the fluctuation of remittance transactions throughout a year. However, resource constraints and legal or institutional problems in direct reporting could pose practical problems for frequent data reporting. A quarterly reporting schedule may be sufficient to satisfy data needs without excessive resource requirements. Some countries may be in a position to implement a reporting schedule with higher periodicity. Irrespective of the frequency of the data collection, MTOs should be able to provide high-frequency data without excessive efforts. For instance, MTOs should provide monthly transactions data covering the reporting period, even if this period exceeds a month.

4.56. Direct reporting of MTOs transactions data allows the gathering of detailed information on remittances, because this information is embedded in MTO administrative records. Aggregate transactions of MTO agents can be generally broken down by the following attributes:

- Date of transaction
- Direction of flows (outbound or inward)
- Country of destination (for outward flows) / of origin (for inward flows)
- Transaction amount
- Transaction purpose

4.57. The desired level of detail of the geographical breakdown varies from country to country and will be usually determined by national and international requirements. Of course, the purpose of payments should also be recorded to aid correct classification of data entries. However, not all countries require that MTOs record the transaction purpose, and the assumption is often made that all transactions through MTOs are personal transfers. In cases where no reliable information on the purpose is available, compilers should seek to verify that these transactions are remittance related. For this purpose, a small survey could be used to establish benchmark data on the stated purpose of transactions through MTOs, including the assessment of transactors' residence and other relevant criteria.

4.58. In addition to the aggregate amount of remittances, the number of transactions can normally also be collected from agents.[38] This allows the calculation of the average amount of remittances, which is a useful variable for modeling approaches and for analytical purposes. Further, basic socio-demographic variables on the transactors, such as nationality, sex, and age, may also be collected if they are recorded by MTOs (which depends on documentation requirements in the compiling economy). Users of balance of payments and of remittances data find tabulations of these data useful for analytical purposes. Therefore, compilers may wish to collect and disseminate these data as a courtesy. These and other data details obtained from MTO direct reporting are also useful complements to other data sources and estimation approaches.

4.59. The reporting rules should clearly state the reporting currency to be used or the criteria to be followed in this respect if more than one currency is used in data reporting. Reporting data in the domestic currency of the compiling economy is the most obvious choice. However, using another currency may be useful if remittance transactions with a dominant partner country take place in that country's currency, or if foreign currency is widely used in the domestic economy. Also, some countries compile balance of payments statistics in currencies other than their own, and it may follow that data reported by MTOs should be denominated in that same currency. For compiling remittances data, the reporting currency is not relevant in itself, but it is important to ensure that there is no ambiguity.

4.60. The reporting rules should also require that both the transaction amount and associated service fees are specified. Reporting MTOs should indicate the total amount paid by remitters, the amount accounted for by all types of commissions and fees (including exchange rate spreads), and the amounts paid to receivers. Commissions, fees, and exchange rate spreads are remunerating the activity of all the involved parties. Therefore, commissions and fees are earned by subagents and agents in two countries (and indirectly perhaps also by the central settlement unit in a third country). An MTO agent in one country may not know the fees and commissions charged by another agent in the partner country. It is therefore not always possible to determine all transactions costs, but reporting agents should at least specify fees and commissions paid in the reporting economy. More detail is usually available because all MTO agents involved in a transaction generally know the net amount that is delivered to the final beneficiary.

4.61. Compilers should ensure that appropriate reporting channels are available that ensure timely responses and limit the reporting burden. Submission of data by

[38]However, the identification of the actual number of "individual" remittances sent may be difficult, because sometimes the sender transfers the remittances of several family members in a single payment.

electronic means, especially through the Internet, ensures fast data transmission and ease in uploading and processing data. In the case of subagents, especially in developing countries or regions with poor infrastructure, reporters should be given more flexibility in order to minimize the burden and encourage reporting. Subagents could report data in any form convenient for them, including hard copies or CD-ROMs sent by mail or courier.

4.62. In most cases, compilers should also standardize the format and software application (or compatibility) that MTOs will use to extract data from their records and report it to the compiling agency. The standardization of data-processing applications ensures that data can readily be uploaded by the compiler and reduces the likelihood of errors in data entry. Exceptions may be considered for smaller MTOs with less developed technology.

4.63. As with all direct reporting schemes, the success of the operation also requires appropriate communication with the reporters. Clear instructions, periodic briefings, and assistance from compilers through a help desk structure can significantly improve the outcome of the activity. Compilers should also have a list of contacts at the reporting MTOs so the queries and data inconsistencies can be addressed quickly and informally. Compilers should strive to establish a productive, trusting relationship with their counterparts at the reporting MTOs.

Institutional arrangements for data collection

4.64. Regulatory aspects related to the MTO channel were discussed in Chapter 2. The type of supervisory authority determines how an agreement between MTOs and the national authorities can be reached to share information. A variety of public agencies, in various countries, have the responsibility to supervise MTOs and other remittance service providers: central banks, financial or anti–money laundering supervisors, local authorities, and custom and tax authorities.

4.65. Although MTOs are subject to some kind of supervision in most countries, this does not guarantee the provision of information useful for compilation purposes. Countries often adopt a regulatory framework directly addressing statistical activities, with a set of statistical regulations. They define the institutions responsible for the various statistical domains, the type of information to be collected, the population of respondents, and their statistical obligations. Sanctions are sometimes imposed for missing or incorrect reporting.

4.66. Central banks (or other banking supervision agencies) have the authority to obtain data from the financial sector, and so banks and other financial intermediaries are obliged to report statistical information on their operations. Consequently, in most countries central banks are able to conduct indirect data collections on MTO payments, through the information on cross-border settlement that banks undertake on behalf of MTOs. The authority to obtain data would extend to direct reporting from MTOs only in countries where the banking or another supervisor has regulatory authority over MTOs. Strict foreign exchange regulations may also make MTOs subject to transactions reporting.[39]

4.67. Countries where the financial regulator (e.g., the central bank) is also a balance of payments compiler and supervisor of MTOs are in a strong position to impose direct data reporting obligations for statistical purposes. This assumes that the regulatory framework permits data to be obtained for statistical purposes, or that information reported for supervisory needs can be adapted for statistical purposes, respecting the relevant confidentiality rules.

4.68. However, in many countries the statistical mandate and the supervisory authority are not vested in the same institution. This may be the case in countries where a national statistics agency and not the central bank compiles balance of payments statistics. National statistics agencies are typically mandated and empowered by a statistics law to obtain data from all relevant resident units. The statistics agency therefore relies on the enforceability of the statistics law, not on supervisory power, to obtain relevant data from MTOs. National statistics agencies also may have direct access to related data sets, such as migration and demographic data, household survey data, and other data sets that are potentially useful for complementing and cross-checking remittances data.

4.69. Before introducing a direct reporting system for MTOs, compilers should confirm that the regulatory or legal powers at their disposal provide sufficient authority to require MTOs to supply all relevant data. The legal provisions have to be broad enough to include detail on transactions and they have to be enforceable. Despite the focus on legal powers, compilers should

[39]Countries with strict foreign exchange rules often have an ITRS. If MTOs are not directly covered in the ITRS, a supplemental reporting system for MTOs would be a useful complement to the ITRS.

Table 4.2. Coverage of Remittance Aggregates Through Direct Reporting by MTOs

Remittance Aggregate	Data Generally Obtainable from MTOs
Personal transfers	Current and capital transfers through MTOs; no data on other modes or transfers in kind
Personal remittances	Current and capital transfers through MTOs; no coverage of compensation of employees or expenditures related to short-term work abroad (travel, taxes, etc.)
Total remittances	Mainly current and capital transfers between households; no coverage of social contributions and benefits or other transactions not solely involving households
Total remittances and transfers to NPISHs	Mainly current and capital transfers between households; very little information on transactions involving NPISHs

Note: When capital transfers between households occur, they are usually larger than current transfers and they may be more likely to be channeled through banks than through money transfer operators (MTOs). Money sent by nonresident workers to their home countries through MTOs may be misclassified as personal transfers.

seek to limit the reporting burden and build a cooperative relationship with all data reporters.

Coverage by type of transaction

4.70. Direct reporting from MTOs as a data source can address only part of the statistical needs related to remittances. The data source is partial by definition because it can provide information only on the payments sent through the MTO channel. This limitation of coverage, even if mitigated by the fact that MTOs in some countries are a very important mode of remittance transactions, must always be taken into account when direct reporting is part of a statistical program to improve remittances data.

4.71. The second relevant characteristic of data obtained from direct reporting by MTOs is that they can provide information mainly on household-to-household payments. Even though potentially they constitute a general purpose payment channel, and therefore can be used by all institutional sectors (firms, government, and so forth), the main activity of MTOs is the transfer of funds between households. This limits the coverage of other items that are required, such as compensation of employees, social contributions and benefits, and transfers involving NPISHs (Table 4.2).

4.72. In summary, direct reporting by MTOs can provide data on personal transfers—that is, current transfers between households, transacted through MTOs. The data that MTOs may provide would exclude personal transfers transacted through banks, informal channels of payment, or in-kind remittances. Direct reporting by MTOs may capture data on capital transfers, although this is less likely because capital transfers are more likely to be channeled through banks.

4.73. The data from MTOs may include data on short-term workers abroad sending money home, although these funds are not personal transfers. These flows could be seen as linked to the concept of compensation of employees less taxes, travel, and other expenses related to short-term employment abroad. It is important that compilers estimate compensation of employees as well as travel, taxes, and other related items on a gross basis.[40]

4.74. MTOs normally carry out transactions in cases where both of the parties are individuals. Therefore, they are not a good source of information on payments of taxes, travel, social contributions, and benefits. Current and capital transfers involving NPISHs and other nonhousehold sectors are also unlikely to be captured. In addition, MTO agents usually do not keep precise records on the specific purpose of a transaction. Therefore, data obtained from MTOs are not easily classified into capital and current transactions and do not permit compilers to separate easily transfers from other transactions. The assumption is often made that most trans-

[40]The potential coverage of compensation of employees less related expenses requires some explanation. In addition to residents (including migrants), the MTO channel may also be used by nonresident short-term workers to transfer funds to their origin countries. The money sent by short-term workers could be regarded as the "net income" of wages less taxes, social contributions, transport, and travel expenses paid abroad. However, MTOs cannot always accurately distinguish short-term workers and resident migrant workers. Furthermore, short-term workers are more likely to take their earnings with them on return to the home country, instead of sending them through institutional channels.

actions passing through MTOs are current transfers, but this assumption may be weak.

4.75. Although MTOs cannot provide data on all remittance-related components (and types of flows), and the classification of transactions is less detailed than compilers would prefer, these data may be useful in estimating current transfers sent by migrants to their country of origin. Although the definitions are not perfectly aligned with those of *BPM6*, data obtained from MTOs can lead to a substantial improvement in capturing transactions by migrants, who account for the bulk of all personal transfers and remittances.

Strengths of direct reporting by MTOs as a data source

4.76. Direct reporting is a promising approach for collecting data on the operations of MTOs with good detail on individual remittance payments. Direct reporting can be used as the main data source in countries where compilers can determine that MTOs are a dominant transaction mode for remittances.

Practicality

4.77. Most countries have a statistics law in place that allows the establishment of direct reporting requirements without further legislation. Reporting requirements can then be established and enforced using the authority of the balance of payments compiling agency.

Cost-effectiveness

4.78. Direct reporting is usually not expensive for reporters and compilers. Although it requires an additional reporting activity, the reporting burden is low and the number of reporters normally is not large.[41]

Timeliness and frequency

4.79. Monthly data are often available shortly after the end of the reference period. Depending on the technological methods used by MTOs to compile and report data, the timeliness and frequency of data reporting can approach that of an ITRS.

Reliability and accuracy

4.80. Data obtained from MTOs are reliable when compared with those from other data sources. Although not all remittance transactions can be captured, those routed through MTOs are in principle fully covered. Some transactions through MTOs may not reflect personal transfers or remittances. Adjustments should be made to data reported by MTOs, where appropriate, for overcoverage and undercoverage.

Compatibility with other sources

4.81. Direct reporting by MTOs is a very useful tool for addressing the weaknesses of other data sources. In particular, the identification of each individual transaction avoids information loss caused by the batching and netting of transactions that affect remittances data collected through an ITRS. Also, the use of detailed MTO data allows a correction of the distortions in geographical breakdown of data obtained from the ITRS. In some countries, thresholds are applied to reduce the statistical reporting burden in relation to small-amount cross-border settlements.[42] Such thresholds often cause significant information loss in relation to remittances, whose amount is typically very small. In countries where the exemption threshold applies only to bank settlements, direct report from MTOs may fill the information gap.

Weaknesses of direct reporting as a data source

Classification errors: Residence of transacting parties

4.82. MTO agents cannot always reliably establish whether payments originate from short-term workers who are nonresident in the country where they originate the transaction or from migrants who are resident there. MTOs ask customers about the place of usual residence or get this information from their identity documents, but a correct assessment, consistent with balance of payments definitions, cannot always be assured. This weakness may imply, for example, that funds transferred by short-term workers to families of origin (who are both resident in the country of origin) are mistakenly included in "personal transfers."

[41]A strategy to reduce reporting costs could be to promote the collaboration between statistics compilers and MTOs at an international level, instead of relying on the information provided by the MTO agents resident in the various countries. In principle, this centralization of the collection of information could allow compilers to obtain more homogeneous and consistent information on the transfers carried out by MTOs across many countries. In fact, a coordinated but relatively modest project could result in useful data for a large number of countries, including some that would not be able to establish direct reporting by MTOs at a national level.

[42]See paragraphs 4.34–4.40.

Classification errors: Purpose of transaction

4.83. Compilers may find evidence that suggests that a significant share of transactions through MTOs are household-to-household transfers, in most cases to the families of origin of the senders. Nonetheless, substantial transaction amounts through MTOs may not be related to remittances. For example, MTOs can be used to make payments related to the purchase of goods or other commercial activity. Also, if a temporary worker sends a portion of his or her income back to the household in the home economy, care must be taken to avoid including this in personal transfers. (The net compensation of the temporary worker should be included in remittances, but the transaction involving the MTO should not be included in transfers, because that would cause double counting in remittances.) Compilers should try to periodically validate the classification of transactions reported by MTOs and may find it useful to establish an adjustment factor for reported data to improve the estimate of personal transfers. An analysis of microdata on individual transactions provided by MTOs would allow an analyst to characterize the distribution of amounts and to establish the adjustment factor.

Problems in establishing effective reporting

4.84. In most countries, the implementation of MTO direct reporting may not pose unusual problems, whereas in others, it may be less straightforward. In many countries, MTOs are not supervised (or licensed) by the financial authorities. Even if they are supervised, in some cases, no useful statistical information is reported by them to the authorities.[43]

Role and concentration of MTOs in the remittance market

4.85. If MTOs are not an important conduit for remittance transactions, direct reporting by them would not provide adequate data for estimating remittances (and may not be an important element in a data source strategy). However, even in countries where MTOs are important, the MTO sector can be so diverse or fragmented that effective reporting relationships are difficult to establish. This could be the case particularly when MTOs have strong regional or ethnic affiliations and little national presence.

C. Surveys of Households

4.86. Well-designed surveys of households can be a valuable source of information for compilers of remittances data. They can be used to improve the quality of data directly, and provide more detailed insights into the nature of flows and their impact because they can provide information on the mode of transaction and the volume and direction of flows. They may be useful as a direct data source, to improve the accuracy of estimates, to better understand remittance flow mechanisms, and to provide estimates of parameters for use in econometric modeling techniques.

4.87. This section of the *RCG* describes methods that may help the compiler obtain data on remittances directly from such surveys. It describes the different options available, including the use of existing surveys and surveys that are specially commissioned. It discusses their strengths and limitations when they are used for balance of payments compilation purposes. However, it does not attempt to provide a full discussion of the methodology for conducting household surveys; for this, many existing reference sources are available.[44]

4.88. It should be noted that household surveys are most commonly used to estimate personal transfers. However, they may also be useful for compiling personal and total remittances; issues relating to the estimation of these items are considered at the end of the section.

Description

4.89. Compilers have several options for using surveys of households. They can survey households that receive remittances, or they can survey households that send remittances. They can use an existing survey, by including specialized questions or modules (Box 4.2), or identify households in the target population. Useful surveys for this approach are usually nationally rep-

[43]See, for example, the work by de Luna Martinez (2005). In particular, using the findings of a survey of 40 central banks of developing countries, Martinez reports that although MTOs participate in the market in 39 out of 40 countries, central banks collect information from MTOs in only 15 countries (38 percent). By contrast, in 40 countries remittances are paid by banks and in 36 of these countries (90 percent) the central banks collect information from them. Moreover, the legal and regulatory framework related to MTO transactions sometimes exclusively focuses on anti–money laundering aspects; for this reason, MTOs are obliged to report only transactions above a certain amount.

[44]For instance, see United Nations (2005a and 2005b). See also the resources available through the International Household Survey Network at www.surveynetwork.org.

Box 4.2. Including Remittance Variables in Household Surveys

Household surveys offer the opportunity to obtain data on remittances and other related social and economic variables (including migration). Although these data are not directly related to the compilation of remittances data in the balance of payments framework, they can be valuable in helping data users understand the relationship between remittances, migration, and factors such as employment status and social background.

Variables that compilers may consider including in their survey of individual remittance senders include:

- Employment status, including self-employed workers, employees (of which: those employed by foreign affiliates and, if possible, intra-corporate transferees)
- Country of residence
- Country of birth
- Length of time in country of residence
- Kind of economic activity of (employing) enterprise (at least distinguishing service industries)
- Level of education

When remittance recipients are surveyed, the survey could seek information on the relationship with the originating party, which could be:

- Relatives who are expected to return to the receiving household
- Relatives who emigrated permanently
- Other individuals
- Government
- Nonprofit institutions serving households
- Enterprises

The purpose for which remittances are made could be broken down into the following:

- Consumption
- Investment in property or a business
- Alimony
- Pension
- Other gifts or donations

Compilers should recognize, however, that adding questions may make the survey more costly, reduce the response rate, and lower the quality of responses. The usefulness of gathering additional data should therefore be balanced against the primary objective of compiling data on the volume of remittances.

resentative and often conducted by national statistical offices. On the other hand, compilers can commission specialized surveys, such as surveys of either those who send or those who receive personal transfers, or subgroups of these populations.

Methods

Estimating receipts using existing surveys

4.90. The use of existing surveys is an attractive option for surveying remittance-receiving households because it is likely to be less costly than mounting a specialized survey, and from the compiler viewpoint it is a much simpler process. Adding questions or modules to a nationally representative sample survey can be done by incorporating the questions within the main questionnaire, or administering a special questionnaire to a subsample of households households that are identified as receiving remittances. For data users, the addition of questions to existing surveys also allows the relationships between personal transfers and other variables collected in the survey to be analyzed and researched. Such surveys are often nationally representative and conducted at regular frequencies, although in some cases the period between surveys is more than one year, which makes them difficult to use to provide direct estimates for balance of payments purposes. In this case, they may be more useful to provide data to cross-check or supplement estimates made from other sources. For many countries, suitable surveys may not exist or may not be conducted on a regular basis. Useful survey types that may be encountered by the compiler are described below, along with some of the issues that arise when using these surveys.

Labor force surveys

4.91. Labor force surveys are often large-scale annual or quarterly surveys with questions related to employment, unemployment, and working conditions. In many countries, they include data on household income. Labor force surveys often include modules on specific topics such as unpaid work, vocational training, labor migration, or remittances.

4.92. The surveys are typically run by a national statistical office or other official body. Many developed countries conduct a regular labor force survey, but relatively few are conducted regularly in developing countries because of resource constraints. The International Labour Organization has recently developed

Box 4.3. Adding Questions to the Ghana Living Standards Survey 2005–06

A module of questions on migration and remittances was inserted into the 2005/06 Ghana Living Standards Survey. This is a large, nationally representative household survey covering 9,000 households; the migration module included 45 questions and was administered to a subsample of 4,000 of these 9,000 households, drawn randomly. The survey included questions on personal transfers for former migrants (those returned in the past five years) and questions on personal transfers (in cash and in kind) from current migrants (see below). The survey included both internal and international migrants, though it was possible to differentiate.

Questions relevant to former migrants currently resident in household

If (NAME) was working or working and studying outside the household, where did (NAME) live and work?

During the last 5 years, for how long did (NAME) live and work outside your household?

When (NAME) lived and worked outside your household, did he/she send money to your household?

How did (NAME) usually send this money to your household?

How much money did (NAME) send to your household per year?

Questions to head of the household about current migrants

Is/are there any household members who is/are currently living outside your household? (list)

For each migrant

At present, where does (NAME) live and work?

How long has (NAME) lived and worked there? (years)

Does (NAME) send any money to your household?

Who in your household usually receives this money?

How does (NAME) usually send this money to your household?

In the past year, how many times has (NAME) sent money to your household?

In the past year, how much money in total has (NAME) sent to (head of household/spouse/others)?

Does (NAME) send/bring goods to your household?

What is the value of goods that (NAME) has sent/brought to your household in the past year?

For all migrants

Since (NAME/S) went outside to work, did you receive remittances from him/her/them for (list, e.g., education, putting up housing unit, etc.)?

a migration and remittances module for use in labor force surveys (the module has already been applied in Thailand and Armenia).

Income and expenditure surveys

4.93. Income and expenditure surveys tend to be large-scale surveys that include questions on either income or expenditure, or sometimes both. In some countries these are annual surveys, but in many countries they occur with less frequency. They are often used to update the weighting patterns in consumer price indices and to produce measures of household welfare. Important examples of these surveys include the European Surveys of Income and Living Conditions (Eurostat), the Living Standard Measurement Study (LSMS), and Integrated Household Surveys conducted in developing countries. LSMS surveys are often infrequent and conducted at intervals of five years or less, and are considered to be part of a subgroup of multitopic surveys. These surveys often include questions on personal transfers and other relevant items as part of the collection of data on income and expenditure patterns, although to collect detailed data a specific module may be added (as, for instance, in the case of Ghana; see Box 4.3). A key advantage of collecting data on personal transfers through multitopic surveys is that links can be made with other variables, such as poverty or other measures of welfare.

Demographic surveys

4.94. Many developed countries run annual general household surveys to collect data on demographic and social variables. They are often less frequently run in developing countries, although two internationally sponsored surveys—the Demographic and Health Surveys sponsored by the United States and the Multiple Indicator Cluster Surveys run by the United Nations Children's Fund—are worth special mention and are run regularly in many countries with the time interval of four to five years. Most demographic surveys do not collect income or expediture data, so they may not be suitable for collecting information on remittance flows directly. However, they may collect data on migration or on the foreign-born population, which may be useful

Box 4.4. The Survey on Overseas Filipinos as a Rider to a Labor Force Survey

The Philippines Labor Force Survey (LFS) is a nationwide survey of households undertaken by the National Statistics Office every quarter each year, to provide information on the labor force and its characteristics. Overseas employment statistics have been compiled since 1993 from the Survey of Overseas Filipinos (SOF), which is a "rider" survey to the October round of the annual LFS. SOF respondents are drawn from the full sample of the LFS and include overseas workers who left to work abroad; overseas Filipino workers (OFWs) are listed in the LFS as members of the household, whether or not they are present in the household at the time of enumeration. The LFS was selected as an appropriate instrument for monitoring overseas employment because it shows the effect of overseas employment on the total employment situation of the country.

As of 2007, the SOF uses the 2003 master sample with a sample size of 51,000 households. This is deemed sufficient to provide reliable information on the number of OFWs and their characteristics at the national and regional levels. The 2003 master sample uses a multistage design, and the sampling frame is based on the Enumerator Area Reference File of the 2000 Census of Population and Housing because it contains the number of households by enumerator area in each *barangay* (the smallest political unit into which cities and municipalities in the Philippines are divided). Sample barangays are selected during the first stage, stratified by the country's 17 administrative regions. Sample enumeration areas are selected for the second stage, and sample households are selected at the third stage in each stratum for every domain. The sampling design results in a self-weighting representative sample of households, where each household has an equal probability of selection.

The survey is conducted through personal interviews with the overseas Filipinos, their relatives, or any member of the household who knows the person who went abroad. It uses a two-page questionnaire containing socioeconomic characteristics (i.e., sex, age, marital status, highest educational attainment, and occupation), place of work abroad, amount of remittances (in cash and in kind), and modes of remittances (i.e., banks, local recruitment agency office, door-to-door, friends/relatives/coworkers, carried on person). A control form is also used to determine the households to be interviewed, such as those with members overseas.

It should be noted that the SOF does not cover overseas workers who have relocated their entire families abroad because they will not be part of the sample. Also, the SOF captures information on only remittances sent, and not the total salary received.

for cross-checking purposes or for deriving parameters for econometric models.

Surveys conducted by private market research companies

4.95. In these surveys, balance of payments compliers may be able to "buy" questions on a specific topic and for a specific target group (e.g., households, or migrants and short-term workers) at relatively low cost. Prices may be set per question, giving compilers flexibility to match costs with their budget, although the number of questions that may be purchased by a single survey client is often limited. In some countries these surveys are conducted with high frequency, so that quarterly estimates can be obtained. Surveys of this kind can also be used by compilers who use ITRS or other non–household survey methods as their primary source of remittances data, because they provide a relatively cheap way of obtaining information about other transfer channels and about transmission behavior (e.g., to determine if hand-carried cash is significant) or the frequency of transfers. Questions and statistical methods are usually designed in close cooperation with the research company. Sampling and enumeration methods (e.g., face-to-face interviews, telephone interviews) vary and particular care must be taken to ensure unbiased and representative results that have statistical validity.

Estimating receipts using specialized surveys

4.96. An alternative approach to using existing surveys is to use the results from specialized surveys of migration, where they exist, or to commission specialized surveys of receivers. In some cases, surveyors may choose to target specific subgroups, such as transfers from particular countries (remittances corridors). Another common approach to sampling is to use an existing survey to develop the sample, by asking a question to identify the household as a member of the target population (see Boxes 4.4 and 4.5 on survey samples in the Philippines and Albania). This approach is most efficient when the target population is evenly distributed throughout the general population.

Estimating payments using existing surveys

4.97. Existing surveys may be able to yield data from sufficient numbers of migrants and short-term workers to enable the estimation of total payments, particularly

Box 4.5. A Specialized Remittance Survey for Remittance Receivers in Albania

The National Survey of Family Remittances in Albania is a multipurpose continuous survey that collects information on a range of topics from households that receive personal transfers. It is commissioned by the Bank of Albania, and conducted by the Albanian Institute of Statistics (INSTAT), to provide information on the volume, origin, frequency, and destination of personal transfers from Albanians living abroad; on the utilization of banking system and money transfer operators for making transfers; and on the use of the transfers by households. Remittances are an important source of income for many Albanian families, with about a quarter estimated to receive personal transfers, mostly from Albanians living in Greece and Italy. The survey is designed to obtain information on the size of inflows, the geographical breakdown of these flows, channels used, how households use the money, the proportion of transfers compared to total household income, frequency of transfers, and the socioeconomic characteristics of recipients. It is designed to be conducted each year, and the sample is a subset of the Albanian Living Standard Measurement Study (LSMS), a nationally representative sample of resident households. The results of the remittances survey are extrapolated to the LSMS survey.

The sample is drawn from the sample of the LSMS survey, which has a two-stage cluster design and a sample size of about 3,600 households. Those LSMS households that are found to have received transfers from the sample for the specialized remittance survey are interviewed by INSTAT using a special questionnaire designed by the Bank of Albania. The questionnaire has five sections: general household information, household income, inflows, use of remittances or savings, and other quantitative questions. Households are asked to estimate average monthly income and to recall total annual receipts for the previous year. Response rates have been very high—close to 100 percent of those households identified—with interviewers often making repeat visits. Survey results were scaled to the resident population of Albania using weights derived for the LSMS. The cost of the survey was around US$28 per household. The survey has provided in-depth data as well as data that can be used to relate remittances to other household characteristics. The survey benefited from the use of personal interviews, which clearly helped maintain high response rates.

Despite the impressive response rates, the major problem with the survey is the underreporting of remittances by households. Responses given by household were not verified against other sources. Other problems encountered were that the household composition was not always the same between the two surveys, because of the difference in timing between the LSMS and remittances surveys. In some cases households had moved in the intervening period. The survey was also very time consuming.

if the proportion of migrants and short-term workers in the population is high. Few countries obtain estimates through this approach, however, because the cost of adding specific questions on remittances in such surveys may be high and the incidence of migrants and short-term workers from specific countries is often too low to enable meaningful estimation of bilateral flows. Countries have, however, used existing surveys to estimate propensities to remit, and have used them in demographic models.

Estimating payments using specialized surveys

4.98. Surveys that target migrants and short-term workers (or households with members who make remittances abroad) are not commonly used to producing estimates of remittances, but are potentially an important and cost-effective data source. Questionnaire content can be carefully controlled, and sample sizes need not be as large as surveys, which are designed to be representative of the whole population. They rely on good sampling design, to be able to identify a relatively rare target population. They may be more suitable in countries where the migrants and short-term workers from a few countries or regions are dominant, or in countries where migrants and short-term workers are known to be clustered in particular regions. They may also be useful in situations where a suitable sampling frame exists.

Design considerations for specialized surveys (payments and receipts)

4.99. The first design consideration for any specialized survey is the population of concern. This could be households who receive personal transfers from abroad, or perhaps more practically, households with members who work abroad, including those engaged in short-term or seasonal work. This population is often relatively rare in the general population; for instance, in the 1990s the proportion of migrants and short-term workers was at most 6.5 percent in three-quarters of all countries. The next consideration is to determine how to generate a representative sample. If a list of households of the target population (or a close proxy) exists, then sampling is straightforward and standard methods can be used based on this sampling frame.

Table 4.3. Illustration of Disproportionate Stratified Sampling: 10 Percent Sample of 280 Enumeration Areas

Stratum	Number of Enumeration Areas	Mean Proportion of Target Population in Each Strata	Proportional Allocation (10% sample) A	Disproportional Allocation B	Adjusted Disproportional Allocation C
1	10	0.1	1	10	5
2	20	0.05	2	10	6
3	50	0.01	5	5	8
4	200	0.001	20	3	9
Expected proportion of target population in sample			0.01	0.06	0.03

4.100. Several surveys, including the New Immigrant Survey in the United States, the Longitudinal Survey of Immigrants to Australia, and the Longitudinal Immigration Survey in New Zealand, have used administrative records of legal immigrants. Some surveys have used other proxy methods to list migrant populations, such as the identification in the telephone book of family names from specific countries. However, in most cases, sampling frames will not be available or sufficiently accurate. There are three main approaches, which are briefly described here: disproportionate stratification with two-phase sampling, snowball or chain-referral sampling, and aggregation point sampling.[45]

Disproportionate stratification with two-phase sampling[46]

4.101. Disproportionate stratification is normally a two-stage process: survey clusters are selected through disproportionate stratified sampling, and then two-phase sampling is used to list households in those clusters that are members of the population being surveyed. The sample can then be drawn from those lists. The idea behind this method is to ensure that sufficient respondents from the population form part of the sample; and that it is possible to assign a probability of selection to each respondent.

4.102. Standard stratified sampling would involve sampling clusters within groups of similar clusters, such as those with similar prevalence of the survey population (i.e., households that send or receive international transfers). However, in the case of a rare population, this may not yield sufficient numbers of population households, so the strata that have the greatest occurrence of population households are "oversampled." Table 4.3 illustrates this method in a stratified sample of 280 enumeration areas (or clusters) where the average prevalence of migrants and short-term workers in the population is 1 percent. A standard sample (column A) would be expected to yield just one household from the target population for every 100 listed; however, a sample that "oversamples" stratum 1 and 2 (column B), in this case using the relative number of the target population in each strata, is expected to yield six households from the target population for every 100 listed, significantly reducing costs. Finally, the statistically optimal allocation recommended by Kish (1965) (where the sample is selected in proportion to the standard error of interest) leads to allocation C when that variable is the proportion of the target population. With care, sample weights can be constructed so that estimates obtained from the sample can be adjusted to give estimates that are representative of the target population.

4.103. The key requirement for this method to work well is the existence of information about the prevalence of the target population within enumeration areas. Countries with strong population registration systems may be able to obtain such information, or it may be possible to construct this information from a recent population census.

4.104. Once the enumeration areas have been selected, the list of actual households in the sample is derived through a two-phase process. This process involves initial listing of households in each area, with a screening process of some kind; for instance, listed households may be asked whether or not they send or receive transfers, or whether or not they are a migrant or short-term

[45]For a full exposition of sampling methods, see Kish (1965).

[46]This is the method recommended in Bilsborrow and others (1997).

worker household. The sample of the target population is then drawn from this screened list. Although this method results in a sample of the target population, it should be noted that identifying a final sample can be an onerous (and often expensive) task because of the listing stage. The two-phase approach was adopted in the case of a specialized remittances survey in Albania (Box 4.5) by screening an existing nationally representative sample used in a large-scale multitopic survey. In this case, disproportionate stratification was not employed because the prevalence of the target population in the overall population is relatively high (about 25 percent).

Chain-referral or "snowball" sampling

4.105. Chain referral is a common method of obtaining samples of rare populations in the absence of good sampling frames. In this method, an initial sample of respondents ("seeds") is identified and is used to obtain referrals to other members of the target population.

4.106. Samples generated from this method have some attractions to the surveyor: there are relatively few prerequisites, and they are cheaper to construct than two-phase samples because there is no intermediate household listing step. However, for these samples to be successful, members of the target population must be able and willing to make such referrals; this is not always the case when surveying migrant groups. Furthermore, the sample will represent the network of linked respondents rather than the target population, and it may be difficult to assign accurate probabilities of selection to respondents.

Aggregation point or intercept sampling

4.107. Aggregation point sampling relies on identifying the target population at specific locations, or "aggregation points." Strictly speaking, this is not a household survey method but a survey of individuals, but the approach has been used widely for surveying rare populations. It usually involves a sampling scheme that selects aggregation points that are representative both geographically and temporally. In the case of estimating personal transfers, migrants could be interviewed as they cross border points, or at other locations they may frequent. The United Kingdom, for instance, conducts a continuous migration survey of this type at border crossings, called the International Passenger Survey. This method was also used in a survey of Ghanaians and Egyptians in Italy, sponsored by Eurostat and carried out by the Netherlands Interdisciplinary Demographic Institute.

4.108. The method is cost effective and may improve the response from individuals who are not often in the household. The approach may be effective in obtaining information on transactions other than transfers. Seasonal workers could, for example, be asked to provide information on both their earnings and their travel expenses. A case study from Bulgaria provides a good example of the multiple data items that can be obtained from aggregation point or intercept sampling (see Box 4.6).

4.109. However, samples can be representative only of those who visit the aggregation points, and there is the potential for bias (for instance, certain groups of migrants and short-term workers may be present at the aggregation points more frequently than others). It is also possible for respondents to be interviewed more than once, and it is important to calculate and apply weights to compensate for this problem. A further disadvantage is that surveys of this type typically have a short questionnaire, because respondents have less time to answer than they would during a home visit.

Remittances captured by type of transaction

4.110. In general, household surveys are normally associated with the estimation of the old balance of payments concept of workers' remittances and the new concept of personal transfers. The measurement of capital transfers, social benefits, compensation of employees, travel and other expenses related to short-term work abroad, and transfers from nonprofit institutions is much less developed. Although it should be possible to estimate some of these items from surveys, there is very limited practical experience at present (see Table 4.4).

4.111. Some problems do arise in the application of standard concepts and definitions. These include the fact that the household concept and the residence rules used in *BPM6* and in migration and demographic statistics do not always match family concepts. For instance, a household member can be absent for more than one year but still be considered by the household to be a member and its main source of income.

Strengths of data obtained from household surveys

Inclusiveness of data

4.112. The merits of using household surveys as a data source for compilers include the potential for collecting data on transfers sent through both formal and informal channels (by asking questions of either the sender or receiver of the funds).

Box 4.6. Estimating the Compensation of Short-Term Workers Abroad in Bulgaria

Large numbers of Bulgarians travel to other countries for short-term work and send remittances through informal channels. This pattern has been triggered by unemployment in Bulgaria and easy access to tourist visas for stays in European Union countries for three months. The Bulgarian National Bank (BNB) uses a model to estimate the "compensation of employees" and "net compensation of employees" that are sent through informal channels to Bulgaria by short-term workers abroad. The BNB uses this model to supplement the data on personal transfers that it collects from an international transactions reporting system.

The BNB obtains monthly information from the Bulgarian Border Police on the number and destination countries of Bulgarians who travel abroad for the purpose of tourism. Many of these Bulgarians are, however, actually traveling abroad with a tourist visa for short-term unauthorized employment. In order to separate the Bulgarians traveling abroad for short-term employment from genuine tourists, the BNB surveys Bulgarian tour operators and estimates the number of Bulgarian tourists using foreign tour operators based on a household survey of tourists. By combining the information on national and foreign tour operators, the BNB is able to estimate the number of Bulgarian tourists traveling abroad, by country. The BNB subtracts the number of Bulgarian tourists from the border police data to derive a monthly estimate of the numbers of Bulgarian workers who travel to other countries for short-term unauthorized employment. The BNB assumes these workers stay for three months because this is the length of their tourist visa. The BNB then estimates the total number of Bulgarian short-term workers abroad in a given month as those who moved abroad that month plus those who moved abroad for the previous two months.

The BNB estimates gross monthly compensation of employees for each destination country by multiplying the estimate of the number of Bulgarians who travel to each country for short-term employment by the monthly minimum wage for that country. When minimum wages were plotted against a comparative price level index, three distinct groups of destination countries were evident, one high wage and high living cost, one medium wage and medium living cost, and one low wage and low living cost. The BNB calculates coefficients representing the cost of living as a percentage of minimum wages for one country, for which detailed information was available on the cost of living, from each of these groups. For high- and medium-wage countries, the BNB used information on the cost of living for students, obtained from financial guides for students. For low-wage countries, the BNB used data on subsistence-level cost of living obtained from official statistical publications. The BNB produced estimates for the expenditures of these workers by applying the appropriate percentage coefficients to the minimum wages of each of the countries in the three groups. Finally, the BNB calculated net compensation of employees by subtracting these expenditures from the gross compensation of employees, by country.

Direct control over data definitions

4.113. In addition, surveyors have more direct control over the information collected, because it is not a by-product of administrative or financial systems. In countries where questions can be added to regular surveys, fresh data on remittances can be obtained whenever the household survey is administered.

Availability of useful circumstantial data

4.114. Surveys can also provide insights about how remittances are transmitted and for what purposes they are used, which can be useful information for the balance of payments compilers when evaluating the coverage of data obtained from other sources. Surveys may also provide information to help estimate bilateral flows.

Weaknesses of data obtained from surveys

4.115. The following general issues need to be understood by the compiler when using data from any household survey.

Sampling error

4.116. There is the possibility of sampling error, particularly where the target population under study is relatively rare and the number of respondent households in the sample is small. The target population may not be uniformly distributed among the population. Special sampling techniques may be needed to identify them and include them in statistically representative samples. In some cases, existing national surveys cover only the household population for whom the sampled address is the main residence. In this circumstance, short-term workers may not be included in the sample.

Non-sampling errors

4.117. There is the possibility of non-sampling error. The most significant error is that information on personal transfers may be underreported, because these data are often considered sensitive by respondents. Households that contain undocumented migrants and short-term workers or receive income from undocumented work-

Table 4.4. Coverage of Remittance Aggregates Through Household Surveys

Remittance Aggregate	Data Generally Obtainable from Household Surveys
Personal transfers	Current transfers reported by households
Personal remittances	Current and capital transfers reported by households, although households may not be able to provide sufficient information for separating current and capital transactions; compensation of employees and expenditure related to short-term work abroad (travel, taxes, etc.) if short-term workers are present
Total remittances	Current and capital transfers to households, including social benefits
Total remittances and transfers to NPISHs	Current and capital transfers to households, including social benefits and transfer to NPISHs

Note: Misreporting may be prevalent in all data items.

ers abroad may be reluctant to participate in household surveys. In some cases, migrants and short-term workers may be excluded from the sampling frame altogether when they are not part of formal households but are living in communal group quarters. Even when households participate, the survey respondent may not report undocumented workers in the list of household members. Questions often require respondents to recall amounts sent in previous periods, which is known to reduce accuracy.

Representativeness

4.118. Samples may not represent the desired target population. In the case of aggregation point sampling, for example, the sample represents the population of all those who frequent locations of the type chosen. If the remittance behavior of this group differs from the whole population, then the resulting estimates obtained in this way will contain a bias. Furthermore, remittances of undocumented migrants and short-term workers are of interest, but they may not be included in samples.

Data compatibility

4.119. Balance of payments concepts and definitions need to be considered when designing surveys or using survey results, and carefully compared to the concepts and definitions used in surveys. For instance, identifying residents and nonresidents may be difficult (e.g., household members who are resident abroad for less than one year may be considered nonresident by the household head), and components required to calculate total remittances (social benefits, pensions, travel expenses) may not be easily collected or identified. Compilers may need to advise surveyors on suitable questionnaire design (for instance, to ensure that the relevant components of remittances can be estimated).

Costs

4.120. The costs of using household surveys vary greatly between countries, in line with the cost of enumeration and the cost of obtaining technical advice. Obtaining estimates with greater precision usually requires larger samples, which increases costs or decreases freshness. Adding questions to an existing survey may be the cheapest method of obtaining household survey data, but resulting usable sample sizes may be small unless consecutive samples are pooled because households making or receiving personal transfers are likely to be relatively rare. Specialized surveys vary in cost according to the sampling method used; the use of disproportionately stratified two-phase sampling is likely to be the most accurate but also the most costly, with chain-referral sampling less expensive, and aggregation point sampling the least expensive.[47]

Overcoming some weaknesses

4.121. Household surveys are likely to be most useful where there are large flows through informal channels, or where data are not available from an ITRS or reporting from MTOs or banks. In these situations the compiler should first review whether household surveys may be useful in estimating remittances for balance of payments purposes; this is best done in conjunction with the central statistical agency. The following checklist may be helpful in this process:

[47]This view is supported by empirical evidence from an experimental survey of Brazilians of Japanese origin conducted in 2006, where a survey of 500 questionnaires was estimated to cost US$142,000 for a random, stratified survey; $67,000 for a chain-referral survey; and $20,000 for an aggregation point survey (McKenzie and Mistiaen, 2007).

(a) Review existing surveys to assess the extent to which they capture information on remittances, and the extent to which they can be used (including the timeliness and periodicity of their data).

(b) Consider the addition of questions on personal transfers and remittances to existing official surveys.

(c) Consider the purchase of questions in multiclient surveys run by private companies or research groups.

(d) Consider a specialized survey of households or individuals or, if specific remittances corridors are very large, a specialized survey of remittance senders in important countries. In the case of surveys of remittance senders, determine whether a suitable sampling frame exists.

(e) Estimate the required sample sizes of remittance senders or receivers, likely response rates, and response bias, given their distribution among the population and other characteristics (pilot surveys may help determine these estimates).

(f) Estimate the extent of other non-sampling errors, such as underreporting or problems in recalling amounts sent or received.

(g) Review the cost of the different options, compared with the potential benefit in terms of improving the estimates of remittances.

(h) In remittance-sending countries, is there a suitable sampling frame that identifies the location of migrants and short-term workers or the foreign-born population?

D. Indirect Data Sources

4.122. The previous sections described the use of direct measurements as data sources for compiling statistics on remittances. Direct measurement relies on an agent, such as ITRS reporters including banks or MTOs, to classify and report transactions routed through them; or on the parties to a transaction, such as households covered in a household survey, to report their transactions. There are situations in which direct measurement of remittance transactions is difficult or impractical. For example, a country may not have an ITRS, and reporting channels other than MTOs may play a dominant role. Household surveys may be too expensive or impractical for institutional or cultural reasons.[48] Hence, the options for direct measurement of remittance transactions are very limited. Data items for which direct measurement is not an option are often estimated based on secondary data.

4.123. This section discusses the use of indirect data sources (also called "secondary data") in estimating remittance transactions. Such estimation processes can be based on a wide variety of secondary data, including existing balance of payments items not relating to remittances, observable economic data, or demographic data. Depending on the nature and availability of secondary data, estimation approaches can be tailored to the needs and possibilities of each compiling economy. Secondary data sources can be used to estimate all relevant remittance items or to fill gaps when data obtained from direct observation are known to be incomplete (see also Chapter 5).

Description of the approach

4.124. Estimation approaches are also referred to as models, reflecting the fact that they are a representation or description of a system or process designed to show its structure or workings. A model's framework is typically based on logic and mathematics. As in other fields, such as the natural and social sciences, models are simplified frameworks designed to illuminate complex processes. This section distinguishes three modeling approaches for estimating flows of remittances:

- Demographic models are based on demographic data. They rely mainly on population registers, administrative data, censuses and population surveys, and surveys of the immigrant population.
- Econometric models are a second approach to estimating remittances. Compilers would identify the determinants of remittances for which data are available, then specify a mathematical model to estimate remittances based on these determinants.
- Residual models rely on accounting identities. These models typically estimate remittances from current account or monetary data and assume that imbalances are explained by unobserved remittance flows.

[48]One would expect that the prevalence of informal transfers would increase the importance of supplementing the ITRS and direct reporting with other data sources or the use of other approaches. If factors such as illegal migration, informal economic activities, avoidance of taxes, or regulations are encountered, households are unlikely to reveal full information in surveys, too. Surveys can be impractical for other reasons, too, including costs, time delay, and complications with statistical methods (such as identifying a relevant population or sample).

Box 4.7. Estimating Personal Transfer (Payments) by the United States

The United States is host country to a large number of migrants and short-term workers, and large remittance flows originate there. However, there are no direct data sources; remittances data are therefore estimated by the United States Bureau of Economic Analysis (BEA) using demographic and household survey data and a model. The BEA assumes that the foreign-born population represents the relevant population of transfer senders in the United States because the foreign-born are most likely to have a personal link to foreign residents. The estimates of personal transfers include all current transfers from resident to non-resident households, regardless of the means of transfer.

The model contains four variables: the foreign-born adult population (on an individual basis), the percentage of the foreign-born population that sends remittances, the income of the foreign-born population, and the percentage of income sent by the foreign-born population as remittances. The foreign-born population and the income of the foreign-born population are based on source data from the United States Census Bureau's annual American Community Survey, a detailed household survey. The percentage of the foreign-born population that send remittances and the percentage of income sent are BEA estimates based on various studies. These studies highlight a variety of demographic characteristics that have a clear impact on sending behavior.

The BEA model assumes that selected characteristics of the foreign-born population (i.e., duration of stay in the United States, family type, country of origin, and gender) affect the percentage of the foreign-born population that sends remittances, the percentage of income sent, and, therefore, the estimates of personal transfers. The model assumes that the percentage of income given remains constant over the duration of stay in the United States, although the percentage differs depending on whether the person sending the remittances has his or her children living with him or her. This assumption permits transfers to vary directly with income, all else held constant. The model also assumes that the percentage of income remitted is significantly higher for persons from less developed countries in close proximity to the United States (especially Mexico and the Caribbean) because the lower costs of migration from these areas allow relatively more poor families to migrate to the United States. And the model assumes that the percentage of the foreign-born population that remits decreases as the duration of stay increases.

To estimate personal transfers, the BEA first arranges countries into four remitting groups, based on each nation's per capita income and proximity to the United States. The four groups reflect different levels of remitting: low, moderate, high, and highest. Using data from the studies mentioned above, the BEA assigns to each group a percentage of income remitted. The percentage of population that remits is held constant across the four groups. The BEA then multiplies the estimate of each country's foreign-born population, arrayed by the demographic characteristics discussed above, by the percentage of the foreign-born population that remits in order to obtain the population of remittance senders. The BEA then multiplies the average per capita income of the foreign-born population by the percentage of income remitted by those who remit in order to obtain per capita personal transfers. Finally, the BEA multiplies per capita transfers by the population of remitters to obtain total personal transfers.

4.125. This section describes each of these three modeling approaches, illustrates case studies of existing models used by balance of payments compilers, and points out the opportunities for devising new models and estimation approaches based on local conditions. Under each of these three approaches, a compiler can distinguish between the modeling of remittances receipts from a given country (credit side) and the modeling of remittances payments to a given country (debit side).

Demographic models

4.126. A compiling country could estimate personal transfers by multiplying the population of remittance senders by an average per capita amount sent. If, however, the country does not have these data available, the country could use demographic data associated with personal transfers to estimate these variables. This section first discusses the merits and challenges associated with using this approach to estimate remittances. It then discusses some of the demographic variables associated with giving behavior. This section also includes case studies that illustrate how compilers from Bulgaria and the United States are using demographic models to estimate remittances (Boxes 4.6 and 4.7).

4.127. As noted in earlier chapters, personal transfers are difficult to measure for several reasons. One reason is that personal transfers are typically characterized by a large number of elusive transactors making small but frequent transactions. Such transactions are difficult to measure using surveys, both because it is difficult to locate the transactors and because it is difficult to obtain reliable responses from them. Another reason is that a substantial portion of personal transfers flows through informal channels, such as the hand delivery of cash, rather than formal channels, such as banks.

4.128. One advantage of a model-based approach that multiplies an estimate of the number of individuals who send remittances by an estimate of their per capita transfers is that it allows a country to capture personal transfers through both formal and informal channels. Another advantage is that estimates can be based on demographic data that are often detailed and timely. The drawbacks of this approach stem from the challenges in measuring the population of senders, who may not always be legal residents, and from data obtained for the other variables, which are typically collected on household surveys and may not be reliably reported by the household.

4.129. In regard to the first drawback, many countries have a large foreign-born population that is difficult to identify and accurately measure, especially when migrants and short-term workers reside in a country illegally. Many migrants and short-term workers are not authorized to work in the country in which they are residing. This leads to several problems when attempting to measure the size of the foreign-born population, their average income, and, ultimately, their personal transfers. This population is difficult to locate and accurately measure; they may be migratory with no fixed address; they may live in group homes in which the total number of residents is unclear; they may have large families that are undercounted; and they may elude survey takers altogether for fear of deportation.

4.130. In regard to the second drawback, compilers face the challenge that migrants and short-term workers may not provide reliable estimates of the amount they send home or their income. For example, it is often the case that migrants and short-term workers underreport their income in surveys of low-income populations. Moreover, migrants may tend to overreport the amount they send home in order to conform with social norms or with their own sense of what they should be sending. Another challenge is that this modeling approach requires frequent surveys of the migrant population on the amount they send home—more precisely the percentage of income sent—and the percentage of the population that sends remittances to ensure the estimates are sensitive to changes in giving behavior over time or to sudden spikes and subsequent drop-offs that may result from significant events abroad such as natural disasters. There may also be significant spikes in cash and in-kind transfers from NPISHs and corporations when a disaster strikes.

4.131. In summary, the accuracy of this approach depends, in large part, on the accuracy of the data reported in household surveys. The accuracy of the survey results will depend on how well the sample represents the general population and the degree to which respondents provide accurate information about their giving behavior. Numerous demographic characteristics are thought to be associated with personal transfers, and there is general agreement on the effect of many of these variables on the amount given. These variables include, among others, country of birth, ethnicity, duration of stay abroad, income, gender, legal status, and the presence of children in the household. Compiling countries that do not collect this type of demographic information might consider using demographic information collected by partner countries as a proxy for the demographic characteristics for their remittance-sending population. The United States model, which is described in a case study, provides one example of an approach for estimating personal transfers sent to households in other countries.[49]

Country of birth or ethnic background

4.132. It is generally assumed that personal transfers are more likely to be made by the foreign born. Therefore, the key demographic information used in estimation models tends to be the size of the foreign-born population. This information is often available from source data. It is possible that compiling economies will need to adjust these data if there are significant transfers by second- and third-generation migrants from certain ethnic groups or if certain parts of the foreign-born population do not engage in this activity. Typically, a model will estimate the size of the sending population based on a percentage of the total foreign-born population. However, it is possible to construct a model that applies data on average personal transfers (including those who do not give at all) to total foreign-born population. Compilers can use households or individuals as the

[49]The United States model is based on variables that are collected by the United States. Compiling countries that have additional data could expand the model to incorporate additional variables that could affect personal transfers, such as number and type of family members in the home country. Countries that do not have the range of demographic data used by the United States could use a model based on the United States approach but with fewer variables.

base unit of the foreign-born population (or adjusted foreign-born population). The choice of base unit is generally made on the basis of availability of data but also has implications for the way in which the model is defined.

Income

4.133. Income is the primary determinant of the capacity to send remittances. Models may use assumptions of the percentage of income that is sent, applied to data on the income of the foreign-born from different countries or ethnic groups, to estimate per capita transfers. The type of data on income available from the source data and used in the model affects the assumptions made about the percentage of income given. For example, if gross income is used in the model, the percentages assumed to be given should be lower than if net disposable income is used. Other key demographic variables that can affect levels of income include gender and the presence of children in the household.

Gender

4.134. When personal transfers are estimated on an individual basis, gender affects the level of income of the remittance sender. Females often have lower average incomes than do males.

Presence of children

4.135. The presence of children in the household increases household expenditures and therefore decreases the available income from which to send remittances. Children also increase the likelihood that migration will be permanent, and shift the economic focus from the country of origin to the household in the host country.

Duration of stay

4.136. The duration of stay in the host country negatively affects the percentage of the population that sends remittances and their amount. Senders who have been in the host country for many years are less likely to give than are those who have recently arrived because connections and obligations to family and friends in the country of origin tend to diminish over time. Although the motivation of the foreign born to send remittances tends to decline with the duration of stay, their capacity to do so often increases because their income tends to increase over time.

Country of origin

4.137. The percentage of income given is likely to vary between different ethnic and foreign-born populations. Generally, this information will be built into any model-based estimation. The percentage of income given is significantly higher for persons from developing countries than for those from developed countries, and it is also higher for those in close proximity to the host country. The percentages of income given by country background can be obtained from large household surveys or targeted small-scale, often academic, studies.

4.138. Compilers could adapt the principles discussed in the previous section and illustrated in the case studies to construct their own models. For example, a compiler could adapt the model for outward transfers as a model for inward transfers by using their own data, or obtaining partner country data, on their adult foreign-born population abroad and that population's average income. If the compiling country chooses to use partner country data, it could be found that a large proportion of personal transfers flows from a limited number of partners. Also, compilers could consider using benchmark data obtained from other countries with similar migration patterns. The compiling country could then use demographic data covering the proportion of the population that sends remittances and the percentage of income sent, adjusted to fit the characteristics of their population, to complete the model.[50]

Econometric models

4.139. An econometric model is a simplified mathematical representation of relationships in the economy expressed as equations. The equations explain how one economic variable can change as a result of changes in other key variables. As a simple example, an econometrician might construct a model to establish relationships between variables, such as remittances and family income, and then use this model to estimate

[50]For example, the United States compilers used a variety of studies, conducted both within the United States and abroad, to estimate the percentage of foreign-born population that regularly sends remittances. The estimates derived from these studies are perhaps applicable to the remittance-sending population in other countries with comparable demographics. Similarly, the United States used a variety of studies to estimate the percentage of income remitted. A compiling country could consider modifying the percentages used by the United States based on the information from these studies and the circumstances of that country. When using third-country data, compilers need to adjust benchmarks to account for the specific features of their own country and ensure that estimation results are plausible.

remittances at different points in time at different levels of income.

4.140. Econometric modeling of remittances may be a particularly useful tool in countries where data collection systems are imprecise. Moreover, a compiler can use econometric models to supplement information from other compilation methods. An econometric model can also contribute to a better understanding of the economic, social, and political mechanisms that determine the volume of remittance flows.

4.141. In order to construct a robust econometric model, a compiler requires data on remittance flows (possibly from an ad hoc survey) and their determinants, and specialized statistical expertise to define the model, to select and employ the appropriate model estimation technique, and to interpret the results.

4.142. In general, the economic variable under study (known as the dependent or endogenous variable) is presented as a function of a number of explanatory (or exogenous) variables:

$$Y = f(X_1, X_2, \ldots, X_k), \qquad (1)$$

where Y is the dependent variable (e.g., remittance flows), X_i ($i = 1, \ldots, k$) are the variables that explain changes in the dependent variable, and f denotes the type of function describing the relationship between the dependent and the explanatory variables.

4.143. In order to formulate an econometric model of remittance flows, an econometrician may use knowledge of social sciences such as economics or sociology to select the determinants of remittances. Mathematical and statistical knowledge is necessary to determine the type of function (f) and the technique to be used to estimate the function.

Determinants of remittance flows (explanatory variables)

4.144. A compiler who plans to construct an econometric model of remittance flows could turn to previous studies as a guide for identifying possible explanatory variables.[51] The relative economic situation in the home and host countries as well as demographic variables related to migration are typically cited as important explanatory variables. Some possible explanatory variables are listed below. As is the case for other types of models, the availability of data for constructing the explanatory variables will depend, in part, on whether the econometrician is building a model to estimate total remittance flows to or from the rest of the world, or whether the econometrician is building a model to estimate remittances to or from a given country (bilateral flows).

- *Income differential:* The income differential between the sending and receiving countries may help explain remittance flows. One would expect this variable to enter the model with a positive sign: the larger the differential, the larger the flows. The ratio of GDP per capita can be used as a proxy for the income differential between sending and receiving countries.
- *GDP growth differential:* In addition, GDP growth differential may also play an important role in determining the flow of remittances because this variable may serve as a proxy for the relative growth potential of the sending and the receiving economies. One would expect this variable to enter the model with a positive sign: the larger the GDP growth differential, the larger the remittance flows, because individuals in the sending country may increase the amount given when they deem their prospects for the future to be relatively favorable.
- *Migration and related demographic statistics:* Bilateral data on stock of migrants and short-term workers for each country pair and related demographic statistics, such as their average duration of stay, gender, and skill level, are possible determinants of remittance flows. For example, because income is strongly correlated with human capital, information about the skill levels of migrants and short-term workers is important.
- *Remittance cost:* Costs vary widely between countries and among institutions involved in the transfer. One would expect this variable to enter the model with a negative sign: the lower the cost, the larger the remittance flows.
- *Rate of return on real estate:* A natural proxy for the return differential on nonfinancial assets

[51]See, for example, Schiopu and Siegfried (2006) and Bouhga-Hagbe (2004). Most studies in the literature on remittances have focused on the estimation of econometric models relating to "workers' remittances" (referring to the concept of remittance transfers used in *BPM5*) credits (receipts) of a given country or a panel of countries. The modelling of the debit side has not been widely pursued. An exception is the work by Faini (1994), who analyzes the determinants of remittance payments by various groups of immigrants resident in Germany. The determinants of remittance flows may differ in models for credits and debits.

would be the bilateral difference in the rate of change in house prices, because sending funds for housing one's family back home is an important reason for remitting.

- *Exchange rate differentials:* Changes in exchange rate in sending or receiving countries may influence the volume of remittance flows.
- *Dual exchange rates:* Existence of dual exchange rates in the origin or destination country may influence choices about the amounts of remittances and their transaction channel.

Building the model

4.145. A simple econometric model describing a linear relationship between remittance flows and their determinants can be expressed as follows:

$$Y = \alpha_0 + \alpha_1 X_1 + \alpha_2 X_2 + \ldots + \alpha_k X_k + \varepsilon, \qquad (2)$$

where Y represents remittance flows (either credits or debits), X_i are the selected determinants of remittances, α_i are the coefficients showing how changes in the determinants influence the remittance flows, and ε is an error term showing that part of Y that cannot be estimated by the explanatory variables. The reference (dependent) variable of the model could be the total remittances sent or received by a country in a given period (time-series analysis) or the remittances sent or received by a country to or from a group of countries in a year or period (cross-sectional or panel data analysis).

4.146. Mathematical transformations of some determinants, such as converting the variables to logarithmic form, might be necessary to guarantee a better fit of the model. A linear model as described in equation (2) might not always be the best option. Depending on the censored nature of the dependent variable and the stationarity of the explanatory variables, other types of models might be considered. Statistical analysis of the determinants (e.g., analysis of issues such as multicollinearity, stationarity, endogeneity, or variability) as well as an analysis of the type of relationship between them and the remittance flows will be necessary in order to select the relevant determinants and the type of model to be implemented. This, consequently, will determine the estimation technique to be applied in order to estimate the coefficients (α_i) and determine the level of remittance flows. Various statistics describing the goodness of fit should be analyzed to determine the best model.

Residual models

4.147. Remittances may also be estimated using models that measure all flows that generate inflows and outflows of foreign exchange other than remittances. Such a model can be based on relevant balance of payments items or monetary data and associated accounting identities. This approach therefore rests on the assumption that, once all observable inflows and outflows have been recorded (including remittances reported through formal intermediaries), discrepancies are most likely unobservable remittances.

4.148. In its simplest form, such a model could then derive remittances as the residual under the assumptions that foreign exchange inflows equal foreign exchange outflows and that all foreign currency inflows are converted to domestic currency for use in the domestic market (see Box 4.8 on a residual model used in Albania). This basic version of the model can be expanded to account for changing cash balances and other observable factors. For example, changes in the cash balances of the financial sector or estimates of household savings in cash can be used to account for temporary imbalances between inflows and outflows.

4.149. A residual model based on monetary data would, in principle, account for all remittances received in financial form, including cash as long as it is exchanged domestically. A residual model based on balance of payments data will identify all remittances as long as goods and services obtained from these remittances (received in cash or in kind) are recorded fully in balance of payments statistics.

4.150. Residual estimations are a low-cost approach to estimating missing data. In principle, this approach accounts for remittances sent through formal and informal channels. It is therefore very attractive for countries with limited resources and scarce alternative data sources.

4.151. However, this approach has severe drawbacks. It relies on the accuracy of data on which the estimation is based. Any errors or omissions in that data will be reported as remittance flows and true errors or omissions remain invisible, making data checks more difficult. For example, an underreporting of exports would automatically result in an overestimation of remittances; because the current account balance remains unchanged, neither error can easily be detected.

Box 4.8. Estimating Remittances as a Residual in Albania

Remittances constitute the largest current account credit for Albania, yet there are few direct data sources. Remittance inflows are received partly through the banking system but mostly through informal channels. The inflows of foreign exchange are converted into the domestic currency, the lek, by banks, bureaus of exchange, or informal markets.

The Bank of Albania (BoA) uses a model that estimates remittances as a residual of inflows and outflows of foreign exchange. The residual inflow serves as their estimate of remittances. The methodology relies on two assumptions: first, recipients convert their remittances to lek for domestic use; second, foreign exchange inflows are equal to outflows (there is no change in the net holdings of foreign exchange outside the banking system).

The following table illustrates how the BoA estimates remittances as a residual:

Inflows		Outflows	
Cash remittances (unknown)	(CR)	Cash imports[2]	(CI)
Cash exports[1]	(CE)	Cash travel (debit)[1]	(CTD)
Cash travel (credit)[1]	(CTC)	Other cash imports in services[1]	(OCI)
Other cash exports in services[1]	(OCE)	Other outflows of foreign exchange[3]	(OOFX)
Other inflows of foreign exchange[3]	(OIFX)		

[1]Not channeled through banking system.

[2]Cash imports are total imports (excluding goods imported as aid, for processing, or financed by trade credit) minus imports that are financed by payments through the banking system.

[3]The net change in the position of foreign exchange holding by banks and bureaus of exchange.

Hence, CR = CI + CTD + OCI − CE − CTC − OCE + NetFX (OOFX − OIFX). Eighty percent of remittances received through banks and financial institutions (RB) are assumed to be converted on the parallel market, and therefore are included in the estimated cash remittances (CR). The remaining 20 percent are not converted; therefore, these inflows of remittances are not included in CR. Hence, the BoA method adds 20 percent to CR to calculate estimated personal remittances (EPR), where EPR = CR + 0.2 * RB.

The EPR, in principle, matches the balance of payments concept of personal remittances. Therefore, the BoA divides this estimate into "personal transfers" and "net compensation of employees" to record these components in the balance of payments accounts by assuming that 90 percent of EPR are personal transfers and 10 percent are "net compensation of employees:"

EPR * 0.9 = personal transfers;

EPR * 0.1 = compensation of employees minus related taxes, social contributions, and transport and travel expenditures.

Note: The applied percentages (90 percent and 10 percent) were estimated based on ad hoc surveys conducted by the BoA at bureaus of exchange and banks.

4.152. Further, cash balances of domestic sectors are often difficult to estimate but are an important component of this model. In many countries, currencies other than the domestic legal tender circulate and are widely accepted for domestic transactions. Therefore, the private sector holds undisclosed amounts of foreign currency. Fluctuations in these cash holdings, if undetected, would result in misalignments of the residual model.

4.153. Perhaps the most fundamental drawback is that the model cannot distinguish between the purposes for which money is sent. Migrants sending money to their country of origin may be supporting family members or they may deposit money in their accounts or purchase assets such as real estate. Cash inflows could also relate to the repatriation of profits from smaller and informal enterprises. All these flows would mistakenly be classified as "personal transfers" by a residual model when in fact investment activities are taking place.

Remittances captured by type of transaction

4.154. Estimation approaches and models can be specified to cover any item; the real constraint is the

Table 4.5. Coverage of Remittance Aggregates from Indirect Data

Remittance Aggregate	Data Generally Obtainable from Indirect Data
Personal transfers	Prime focus of many residual and demographic models
Personal remittances	Personal transfers, compensation of employees, and expenditure related to short-term work abroad are estimated by some approaches
Total remittances	Social benefits and transfers involving NPISHs could be estimated; actual transactions data may be available but not separately identified
Total remittances and transfers to NPISHs	Social benefits and transfers involving NPISHs could be estimated; actual transactions data may be available but not separately identified

Note: Any transaction can, in principle, be estimated indirectly.

availability and reliability of source data (see Table 4.5). In practice, estimations are more frequently used to obtain data on items that are difficult to measure directly (and the *RCG* recommends that direct measurements be used where feasible). The use of estimations on the basis of indirect data is probably most useful for transactions involving households and individuals. Transactions by households and individuals, especially when operated through unofficial channels, are more difficult to measure directly.

Strengths of estimates based on indirect data

Universal coverage

4.155. Estimations can cover remittances sent through formal and informal channels.

Low costs through use of existing data

4.156. Indirect data are often available without further costs (especially if they are based solely on readily available administrative data), and estimation procedures are typically not expensive. The estimates can be based on demographic data that are detailed and timely in some countries. However, if additional data have to be specifically obtained (e.g., through surveys), costs can be substantial.

Flexible data specifications

4.157. Model-based approaches are flexible. Compilers can design models to fill gaps in data sources or to provide global totals. For example, compilers may have reliable data for remittances sent through financial institutions but not through other channels. One could construct a model to estimate the remittances through these channels. In another case, compilers may have data covering remittances sent to one partner country but not to all other countries. One could construct a model to estimate remittances to all the other countries. Further, estimation methods can be designed to measure a specific type of remittances in conformance with the balance of payments definition, such as personal transfers or personal remittances.

Bilateral data may be obtainable

4.158. If census- or survey-based data of the remitters' economy of origin are available, good-quality regional and partner country estimates may be obtainable.

Econometric models promote a deeper understanding of remittances

4.159. Estimated coefficients of econometric models enable a better understanding of the relationship between relevant economic, social, and political factors and the remittance flows. These factors are represented by the model's explanatory variables. However, econometric models depend on good-quality raw data, which can be difficult to obtain.

Estimates are reasonable

4.160. Model-based approaches can often ensure that the estimates of remittances are within reasonable bounds. For example, models that estimate remittances based on information covering the population of remitters, their income, and an assumption on their propensity to remit can ensure that per capita remittances are reasonable.

Weaknesses of estimates based on indirect data

Source data remains critical

4.161. Only reliable input data can lead to sound estimates, regardless of the sophistication of an estimation method or econometric model. Demographic models, which often rely on estimates of the migrant population, suffer from weaknesses in demographic input data. Econometric models depend on the quality of the data on remittances (such as the dependent variable). Shortcomings with an econometric model's explanatory variables, such as measurement errors and the degree to which they are correlated, can lead to inaccurate coefficients and affect their statistical significance. Residual models are most susceptible to input data weaknesses and will distort data if there are errors or omissions.

Assumptions are not verifiable

4.162. Indirect data are converted to remittance estimates using a set of assumptions. These assumptions should be plausible, but it is often not possible to test or verify them in practice. Moreover, assumptions are often fixed over long periods and therefore do not reflect changes over time.

Results are often not verifiable

4.163. Because models are specified in such a way that their estimates are plausible, it is often difficult to verify their results.

Residual models

4.164. Residual models are extremely sensitive to measurement errors of the other flows and misspecifications in underlying assumptions. A change of assumptions alone can often change remittance estimates substantially (and there may be no firm basis for choosing between assumptions). Misclassifications are also likely to occur because a residual model esti-

Table 4.6. Summary of Data Source Characteristics

	ITRS	Direct Reporting	Surveys	Secondary Data
Cost-effectiveness	Low costs if an effective international transactions reporting system (ITRS) is already in place	Reasonable costs if number of required reporters is limited	Household surveys are costly; lower-cost approaches can provide useful data as complement to other sources	Much secondary data are freely available but compilation may require additional surveys
Timeliness	Very timely if adequate reporting and data-processing facilities are used	Reasonably timely, depending on reporting infrastructure	Surveys typically take time to conduct and to process	Very timely if data used are timely
Frequency	Very frequent if adequate reporting and data-processing facilities are used	Quarterly reporting is achievable with sound reporting infrastructure	Frequency is often not optimal, mainly because of costs	Frequency depends on the choice of source data
Accuracy	Accurate within the limitations of coverage (with adequate coding and processing procedures)	Good accuracy of covered transactions if properly classified	Accuracy often disappointing, with underreporting as a result of recall and other problems	Potentially lower accuracy than other methods; lack of direct measurement and of data checks
Coverage	Transactions through some channels only; poor coverage with a high reporting threshold; poor coverage of compensation of employees and travel-related items	Good coverage of transactions through the channel covered	Depends on survey design; covers all channels and all types of remittances if well designed; good coverage difficult to achieve	Variable; depends on type of data and local circumstances
Conformity with definitions	Reasonable, but good classification of transactions may be difficult to achieve	Good, but proper classification of transactions may be difficult to achieve	Very good, but depends on survey questions and enumeration	Average to low because secondary data sources often follow different concepts
Other risks and constraints	High demands on regulatory and institutional environment; at risk from exchange liberalization	Legal environment must support reporting requirement	No proven methodology; low response rates; underreporting	Use of data in estimation models depends on unverifiable assumptions; lack of cross-checking

mates the volume of flows that escaped observation but does not provide information on the purpose of the transaction or the parties to the transaction.

Bilateral data are not always reliable

4.165. To the extent that models rely on ITRS data, the regional and partner country breakdown will likely be distorted as a result of settlement through financial centers.

E. Summary Table

4.166. Direct measurement of remittances—through transactions reporting or surveys—may be considered preferable to estimating data from indirect sources as long as measurement is feasible. Factors such as the costs of measurement, the timeliness of obtaining data, and legal and institutional factors determine whether direct measurement is feasible.[52] If any factors strongly discourage direct measurement, estimation and modeling approaches can present themselves as the more practical approach.

4.167. In practice, compilers will often not choose between different data sources for remittances but instead combine different sources and estimation methods to achieve better coverage. This means that direct measurements will be used where practical and they will be supplemented by estimates where they are not.

4.168. To guide compilers in choosing approaches and data users in interpreting results, this section summarizes the merits and drawbacks of all approaches and provides a comparison in tabular format (Table 4.6). The table displays the most typical characteristics of different data source approaches against important criteria. It should be noted that such a summary omits much useful detail and the table cannot do justice to all different circumstances and examples of using different data sources. Users of the *RCG* are therefore advised to consult the relevant chapters on each source and use this table as no more than a reminder of the main findings.

[52]For instance, legal factors determine whether transactions reporting is enforceable, and cultural factors determine whether surveys are likely to yield credible data.

CHAPTER

5 Compilation and Data-Processing Issues

5.1. This chapter discusses the limitations of reliance on a single data source, the combination of data from multiple sources in compiling all relevant remittance aggregates, and the use of secondary data for estimating missing components such as specific informal remittance flows or adjustments. It outlines a comprehensive approach to improving remittances data and also discusses the problems arising from a misalignment of definitions with data classifications. In most aspects, compiling remittances data is not substantively different from compiling data on other balance of payments items (the more specific problems lie in obtaining adequate data). Therefore, this chapter briefly discusses compilation issues that apply more generally. However, this chapter also draws attention to the database and computing requirements that some approaches may bring.

A. General Compilation Issues

5.2. The tasks of data compilation include the extraction of data from various collections (such as migration data, administrative data, surveys, and reporting systems), processing and compilation of balance of payments accounts and supplementary series, and data management as well as the critical evaluation of data sources and the assessment of data quality. Extracting data requires judgment; compilers have control over some data sources (e.g., an MTO direct reporting system under their control) but also need to evaluate the usefulness of data sources that are not under their control (e.g., administrative data available from government departments). Both the technical tasks of storage and manipulation of data and the critical assessment of data quality are important. Compilation requires sound judgment in the evaluation of data sources and estimation methods. Judgment is particularly important for compiling remittances data because there is no single reliable data source.

5.3. The DQAF sets out good compilation practices applicable to all items, including those related to remittances.[53] The selection of adequate data sources and assessment of source data are important aspects of ensuring the accuracy and reliability of balance of payments data. Other important factors are the selection of appropriate statistical techniques, the validation of intermediate results and outputs, and revision studies. Further, the serviceability of statistics depends on factors that include the periodicity and timeliness of data, its consistency, and revision policy and practice.

5.4. Sound source data are measured by different factors, such as the following: data are obtained from a comprehensive data collection program that takes into account country-specific conditions; they reasonably approximate the definitions, scope, classifications, valuation, and time of recording required; and they are timely. Further, the DQAF requires that source data are routinely assessed so that errors, omissions, and other problems can be identified and addressed.

5.5. Statistical techniques cover both compilation procedures and adjustments made to raw data. Compilation procedures should ensure that errors are minimized and that ancillary and benchmark information is used where possible. Sound adjustments must also be employed to make source data consistent with balance of payments requirements. This may include adjustments for definitional differences (e.g., ITRS data capturing net settlement data instead of gross transactions) or estimating missing observations (e.g., underreporting in a household survey). Also included are procedures used to incorporate unrecorded activities, including remittances through informal channels.

[53]Readers are advised to consult the DQAF for further details. The *RCG* will summarize only the most important points. See Appendix 2 for the generic DQAF.

5.6. The validation of intermediate results and final outputs ensures that data are plausible and consistent with other data and relevant information. Compilers who do not use demographic data as the main input are therefore advised to use any available data on migration to verify the plausibility of remittance estimates. Other data sets, including monetary data, can also be used to cross-check remittance estimates derived from other data. Discrepancies in data or counterintuitive results should be investigated.

5.7. From time to time, compilers may need to revise previously released data (including preliminary data). Reviews of revisions should be carried out to ensure that they are not showing a trend. If a trend is discernable (e.g., if preliminary data tend to underreport remittances), estimation techniques should be adjusted.

5.8. The periodicity and timeliness of remittances data should follow that of the overall balance of payments compilation in each country. This implies that the requirements of the applicable dissemination standard are being met.[54] Compilation systems that rely on household survey data for their remittances data are likely to face problems in obtaining sufficiently timely and frequent data. Estimations may then be used for compiling preliminary data that will be adjusted once household survey data have been processed.

5.9. Remittances data should be consistent with the standard presentation of the balance of payments. This applies to standard items as well as supplementary components, which are "constructed" from elements of standard components. Remittances data should also be reconcilable with national accounts data and consistent with relevant demographic data. Inconsistencies should be investigated.

B. Using Data from Diverse Sources

5.10. Remittance transactions are heterogeneous and no single data source can ensure that all transactions are reported adequately. Data obtained from the ITRS and direct reporting from MTOs capture only transactions routed through the respective formal sector institutions. Surveys are subject to underreporting and misclassifications. Also, survey data may be less timely and frequent than data obtained from other sources. Administrative data are collected for purposes other than compiling remittances data, so neither its coverage nor definitions may be well aligned with balance of payments data needs.

5.11. Given the shortcomings of each individual data source, data from different sources may be combined. Additional data or estimates may be required to account for transactions passing through channels not captured by the main data source (an example, based on combining direct reporting with an ITRS, is presented in Box 5.1). Also, a frequent and timely data source such as an ITRS may be used to compile regular preliminary data, while a less timely but perhaps more accurate source, such as an annual survey, would be useful in revising these data. Compilers therefore have a need for data from numerous sources to ensure sufficient accuracy, coverage, timeliness, and frequency of output data. Compiling data on remittances may be more demanding in this regard than many other balance of payments items would be.

5.12. Secondary data may be used to estimate data items for which no data are readily available (see Chapter 4). These estimates may cover the aggregate of a line item (e.g., personal transfers) or just a subset of transactions not covered by another data source. For example, one country may choose to base its estimates of personal transfers entirely on secondary data because no direct measurement approach is feasible. Another country obtains data on personal transfers from its ITRS, but complements these data by estimates of personal transfers routed through informal channels not covered by the ITRS. A third country uses household surveys as a primary data source but uses estimates to adjust the results for underreporting of remittance receipts by households. An example of using partial data obtained from direct reporting in a data model is outlined in Box 5.2.

5.13. Estimates can therefore either replace or complement direct measurement. In either case, it is important to ensure that using data from two sources for the same item will not lead to double counting. For example, a country could use data from its ITRS as a main source for all balance of payments items but complement these data by direct reporting from MTOs for personal transfers. Although the MTOs will then report all their relevant transactions, the ITRS would still capture net settlement data related to MTOs' activities. Appropriate adjustments to the

[54]However, it is feasible to compile the supplementary items (especially "total remittances" and "total remittances plus transfers to NPISHs") less frequently and timely because these data are less important for macroeconomic management and surveillance.

Box 5.1. Combining Direct Reporting with an ITRS

Many disadvantages of the use of an ITRS for compiling remittances data arise from its limited coverage regarding transactions that are settled only on a net basis or that bypass formal settlement structures entirely. Compilers who plan to rely on an ITRS as their main data source should contemplate complementary data sources to compensate for the limitations of the ITRS. Direct reporting by MTOs can provide data on gross remittance transactions, with a reliable geographical breakdown, as opposed to net settlement data. Household surveys can provide data on transactions that an ITRS cannot measure, such as compensation of employees earned abroad or transactions through informal channels. Administrative and other secondary data can be used to estimate any missing components. Models can also be employed as an auxiliary means of controlling the accuracy of data obtained from an ITRS. Econometric forecasts of remittances may be used to check the plausibility of the data obtained from an ITRS. Because ITRS data are very timely, other actual sources are often not available for cross-checking.[1]

In combining data obtained from MTOs and data from the ITRS, double counting will occur if MTO settlement transactions are not omitted from bank transactions. Data reported by MTOs should replace (and not be added to) the transactions initiated by MTOs and reported by banks in the ITRS system. In order to facilitate cross-checks with bank reports, MTOs should separately identify their settlement transactions through resident banks, with sufficient data to allow a reconciliation between the two data sets.

If compilers wish to identify the partner countries of remittance transactions for the compilation of bilateral data, direct reporting can be a useful complement to data obtained from an ITRS or other sources. It has been noted that partner country data on remittances obtained from the ITRS often reflect the settlement country, not the true partner country. From direct reporting, compilers can obtain benchmark data for partner country attribution, which can be applied to data from other sources. For instance, information obtained from MTOs can be used to adjust the country distribution recorded by the ITRS.

[1]An example of econometric forecasting is presented in Bank of Spain (2006).

ITRS data must be made to exclude MTOs' settlement transactions (see Box 5.1).

5.14. Depending on the nature and availability of secondary data, estimation approaches can be tailored to the needs and possibilities of each compiling economy. Estimates of relevant remittance-related transactions can be based on data such as migration records, other demographic variables, labor statistics, social security records, travel or transportation data, or any other data set that is readily available and reliable. Methodologies involving estimation can be used to estimate all relevant remittance items or to fill gaps when data obtained from direct observation are known to be incomplete (e.g., a compiler may decide to use an estimation methodology for all transactions recorded as "personal transfers" while the compiler's colleagues in another country obtain data from MTOs but estimate data on "personal transfers" passing through channels other than MTOs). Both approaches may provide good quality estimates, but compilers should endeavor to use data obtained from direct measurement wherever feasible, at least as a plausibility check of model-based estimates, and to adjust and supplement these data as necessary.

5.15. Work plans for improving remittances data often focus on measuring or estimating compensation of employees and personal transfers. However, the compilation of "personal remittances" also requires the estimation of travel, transportation, social contributions, and taxes related to short-term employment abroad. In a few cases, direct measurement for these items may be possible. For example, detailed administrative data related to short-term workers in some countries may document the social contributions made by nonresident workers. However, in most cases, direct measurement is not feasible.

5.16. Of course, these data are all subsets of larger items. Travel and transportation related to short-term employment are part of overall travel and transportation services. Social contributions and taxes are part of larger totals. It is difficult to estimate the share of travel, transportation, and transfers attributable to short-term workers. In most cases, a more robust estimate can be derived from estimates of the number of nonresident workers leaving or entering a country, their length of stay, earnings, and subsistence costs. These data are themselves often estimates, but numerous data sources including partner country data are frequently available. Compilers may wish to consult unusual data sources.[55]

[55]The case study from Bulgaria provides some examples. For example, the Bulgarian compilers approximated the living costs of Bulgarian seasonal workers in European Union countries by refer-

Box 5.2. Direct Reporting as Input to a Data Model

Data obtained from MTOs may be useful to estimate a model for remittances based on data from surveys, censuses, and population registers. For example, a simple model for the estimation of remittance outflows is the following:

$$R = \sum_{i=1}^{J} r_i a_i n_i N_i ,$$

where

- R is the estimate of the total remittance outflows;
- r_i is the average amount per remittance sent by the households of a given nationality i ($i = 1, \ldots, J$), during a given reference period; this information can be obtained from MTO direct reports (assuming that the average remittance amount is similar regardless of transaction channel);
- a_i is the proportion of households of the given nationality that send remittances; this information can be obtained from a household survey of remittance senders;
- n_i is the average number of remittances sent by households of the given nationality (excluding households that do not send remittances at all); this information can also be obtained through a household survey;
- N_i is the size of the population of households of the given nationality living in a country; this information can be obtained from censuses or population registers.

Similarly, the information on the amount transferred from a given country using MTOs may be combined with the following additional information obtainable from a household survey (which together define the "propensity to use the MTO channel"):

- The proportion of persons who send remittances and, within the latter group,
- The proportion of persons using the MTO channel.

This would allow estimating the aggregate amount of remittances sent from a given country through any channel, formal or informal. The "propensity to use the MTO channel" could be used as a benchmark (and would be updated only infrequently) while regular data from MTOs could be grossed up for timely and frequent estimates of total remittances. With appropriate benchmark data from the household survey, the model can also be used to estimate aggregate remittance inflows.

Any estimates should then be compared with the larger item of which they are a part. Other plausibility checks, as well as comparisons with important partner countries, are also advisable.

C. A Comprehensive Approach to Improving Remittances Data

5.17. The large number of remittance transactions and the multitude of channels pose challenges to the compilation of comprehensive statistics. This section deliberates on a practical approach toward building a work program for improving remittances data, with due consideration to reporting burden and compilation cost.

Step 1. Understand the current situation

5.18. Compilers wishing to improve remittances data first need to understand the current situation regarding personal remittance transactions, focusing on two factors: identifying possible remitting channels and recognizing the predominant remitting channels used in the country among those possible channels. If the compiler is not acquainted with the situation, it is necessary to gain an understanding by means of conducting sample surveys; interviewing banks, MTOs, credit card companies engaged in money transfer, and the regulatory authorities; or making estimates based on relevant statistics. Household surveys are often useful for identifying the relative importance of remitting channels. Sometimes, valuable information can be obtained from surveys and investigations carried out by others, such as international organizations or academic researchers.

5.19. Interviews with banks and money transfer organizations, or other agencies delivering remittances, are useful to identify their role in the intermediation of remittances in the country. Interviews with supervisory authorities provide ways to understand the importance of banks and money transfer organizations in the relevant country from the institutional point of view. Existing statistics that may provide a clue to the scale of the remittance channels should also be used to get a broad understanding.

encing the estimated living costs of students, which are published by universities.

Step 2. Evaluate current data collection system

5.20. Compilers should then evaluate the current data collection system on remittances in the balance of payment statistics. By comparing the major remitting channels and the data collection system identified, compilers can check the match between important channels and data sources covering them, identifying the most important omissions. For the channels that are insufficiently covered in the current data collection system, compilers can assess their relative importance.

Step 3. Prioritize

5.21. A sound compilation strategy needs to prioritize tasks by taking into account data needs, including the coverage, accuracy, timeliness, and periodicity of data, as well as the costs of improving data (this includes an assessment of the need for improved remittances data versus other data needs and the capacity of the compiling agency to implement improvements). The channels identified as being insufficiently covered in step 2 are the targets for the expansion of the coverage.

5.22. Remittances are made through various channels. Improving coverage carries costs that vary depending on the channel and can be large in terms of reporting burden, human resources, and finances. Although full coverage of all remittance channels would be ideal, it is probably unrealistic. Therefore, compilers should identify the important channels and expand data sources strategically. When data cannot be obtained for important channels, estimates should be developed based on the best available benchmarks and indicators.

5.23. Other aspects of the quality of statistics, such as accuracy, timeliness, and periodicity of source data, should also be examined along with the reporting cost. Prior consultation must be held to decide the minimum requirements of data quality. If most of the remitters in the country tend to use a particular channel, the compiler should try to improve the data quality of that channel, whereas improvement of other minor channels may be kept to a modest degree.

Step 4. Improve and expand data by channel

5.24. Different data sources and approaches cover different channels and transactions. Compilers should therefore improve and expand their data source program with specific reference to data gaps and omissions in existing source and priorities identified in step 3. Different data sources are suited to different channels (as discussed in Chapter 4):

- ITRS and direct reporting from banks may be an effective data source for remittance transactions through banks.
- Direct reporting is a good approach to obtaining data from MTOs provided that a supportive legal environment exists, including a registration and reporting requirement for MTOs.
- Household surveys can be effective in capturing data on earnings abroad of short-term workers and on other remittances through informal channels.
- Other data sources, including administrative and demographic data, are a good basis for estimating transactions that cannot be directly measured.

5.25. The effective ways to capture data depend on the major remitting channels as well as whether the country is the remitting country or the recipient country. For example, it is generally easier to identify remittances in ITRS data in the remitting than in the receiving country, because banks cannot easily determine the transaction purpose when crediting accounts. On the other hand, it may be easier for the recipient country than for the remitting country to conduct household surveys on remittances because of sampling problems related to remittance-sending households. Therefore, compilers should understand the situation of the country, identify their specific data needs, and choose effective ways for improving and expanding their source data.

D. Database Management and Computing Requirements

5.26. Timely, efficient, and reliable data compilation relies on adequate infrastructure for entering, processing, and checking data. Data on remittances may not pose unusual challenges in these areas, but some compilation approaches make higher demands than others.

5.27. If data on remittances are obtained from an ITRS and details on every transaction are individually reported regardless of amount (i.e., if there is no threshold), the amount of data to be entered and processed can be very large. In some countries, the high reporting and processing burden was addressed by applying reporting thresholds. While reducing the data volume, such thresholds also cut out much relevant data on remittances. ITRS systems that have no thresholds but do have sufficient reporting detail and fast, reliable electronic data transmission, are well suited for compiling remittances data; those without these attributes are less adequate. Detailed direct reporting by MTOs shares many features with a full ITRS. Large amounts of data may be reported, but automation can ensure fast and reliable processing.

5.28. Household surveys can also collect large amounts of data. Coding and entering data are both resource intensive and prone to error. Some compilers outsource some functions related to enumeration, coding, and data entry. Surveys are, in most cases, demanding in terms of staff, logistics, and other real resources.

5.29. Data models for estimating remittances from secondary data can range from simple to highly complicated and data intensive. Higher complexity does not necessarily result in greater accuracy. Adequate models can be built using simple desktop applications. The reliability of data models is largely determined by the quality of underlying data and their assumptions.

CHAPTER

6 Dissemination Issues

6.1. This chapter reviews good practices in disseminating data on remittances. Because these data are part of the balance of payments framework, general guidance on the dissemination of balance of payments data applies and some important aspects are summarized. However, this chapter also draws attention to issues that are specifically important to data on remittances, including the dissemination of supplementary information, the importance of bilateral data to some users, the dissemination of data to users who are not otherwise users of balance of payments statistics (and may not be economists), and the dissemination of data and metadata from experimental compilation exercises.

A. General Dissemination Issues

6.2. The *RCG* guide covers data on remittances in the balance of payments framework. In compilation as well as dissemination, best practices applicable to the balance of payments statement in general are also applicable to data on remittances. The DQAF provides guidance on the aspects of good practice in data dissemination.[56] Important elements of good dissemination practices include data accessibility, metadata accessibility, and adequate assistance to data users (see Box 6.1).

6.3. Data accessibility includes the choice of adequate media and formats of dissemination, data release on a preannounced schedule, and access to data for all users at the same time. Balance of payments data are often released in regular statistical bulletins published by the compiling institution. These are often accessible both in print and on the Internet. Press releases or briefings for specific target audiences are often made available at the date that data are published. It is desirable that data release dates are set in advance and communicated to interested users (e.g., by publishing a data release calendar) and that all users gain access to data at the same time to prevent the abuse of insider knowledge. Most countries also report their data for inclusion in *International Financial Statistics* (*IFS*) and the *Balance of Payments Statistics Yearbook* (*BOPSY*), which are published by the IMF. These publications tend to be less timely than domestic data publications but provide comparable data from many countries and reach a wide audience.

Box 6.1. User-Friendly Data Dissemination: The Example of the Banco de Portugal

The Banco de Portugal, Portugal's central bank, improved its data dissemination system in January 2006. Since then, online access to the Banco de Portugal's Statistical Interactive Database has been available to all users through the Internet. This service ("estatisticas online") is user friendly and is accessible through Portuguese and English language sites. It provides easy navigation and access to the following:

- data in a time-series format;
- data in a multidimensional format;
- data and metadata on the statistics compiled by the Banco de Portugal (and by other institutions, with links to the relevant sites);
- the possibility of personalizing users' search options and registering for alert messages (notifications by e-mail on updates of prior selected data series); and
- a glossary, a release calendar, and a help facility.

Regarding remittances, the website provides easy access not only to transaction totals but also to bilateral data regarding a wide range of counterpart countries. This interactive database is called Bpstat. The Portugal's central bank website is www.bportugal.pt.

[56]This chapter summarizes only the most relevant points made by the DQAF. Compilers who wish to devise a dissemination strategy for remittances data are advised to consult the *RCG* together with the full DQAF.

6.4. Metadata accessibility requires that sufficient information is available on the concepts, classifications, and statistical techniques used in compiling balance of payments data. Metadata should also highlight data shortcomings, omissions, and deviations from international standards and practices, especially on definitions and classifications. Metadata should enable data users to understand the contents and limitations of associated data and allow them critical, well-informed use of these data.

6.5. Assistance to data users is important in case data users have problems accessing or using data. Contact points should be published, and data users should be able to obtain prompt and knowledgeable service. Information about related data series should be available through a publications catalogue.

B. Standard and Supplementary Components

6.6. The *RCG* discusses various data items (their definitions are covered in Chapter 3). Some of them—notably "compensation of employees" and "personal transfers"—are components of the standard presentation of the balance of payments and are therefore part of any release of balance of payments statistics. Other items discussed here are supplementary items whose compilation and dissemination is encouraged but voluntary. If they are compiled, they should also be released through normal channels, such as a statistical bulletin.

6.7. Press releases or briefings for specific target audiences often focus on key items. Whether data on remittances should be included depends on the intended audience and the importance of remittances to the economy. If remittances are to be included, both standard and supplementary items may be used to illustrate recent developments in the reporting economy; however, it should be ensured that the audience understands that supplementary items are not part of the standard presentation.

6.8. Data reported for inclusion in the *BOPSY* and the *IFS* do not include supplementary items. However, both standard and supplementary items may be of interest to other data releases by international organizations. National statistical publications are likely to be the main dissemination channel for supplementary data, including items on remittances. Supplementary data referring to remittances could also be disseminated through publications or websites dedicated to remittances data or related topics, such as migration.

C. Bilateral Data

6.9. Balance of payments data are normally compiled and disseminated by the reporting economy in a format that shows all transactions of residents with nonresidents, regardless of the country of residence of the nonresidents. This mirrors the convention in compiling national accounts data where the "rest of the world" account represents all nonresident entities.

6.10. For bilateral data, compilers have to identify the residence of the nonresident party—that is, they have to know the partner country to each transaction. Such bilateral data represent specific compilation challenges. Data sources on the residence of the foreign counterpart in every transaction have to be identified and additional data have to be processed. Often, it is difficult to establish the residence of the foreign counterpart if transactions are settled through third countries or transactions wholly take place in one country (e.g., travel services).

6.11. However, bilateral data are compiled and disseminated for some important data series. One that has geographic detail is the *Direction of Trade Statistics*, published by the IMF, which provides quarterly and annual estimates of bilateral trade data. Numerous countries also provide balance of payments data with major partner countries.[57] Bilateral data are not in all cases analytically relevant and can sometimes mislead data users. However, remittances are often closely related to migration between two countries, and bilateral remittance flows are therefore an analytically useful data item. In fact, data users often search for bilateral data as a meaningful measure for demographic and economic phenomena.

6.12. The dissemination of bilateral data should therefore be part of the longer-term work program of compiling agencies. Bilateral remittances data do not need to include all partner countries. Instead, bilateral data should focus on important remittance corridors—that is, pairs of countries with large flows. Relevant corridors can often be identified using demographic data (see Box 6.2). For most countries, a small number of corridors are likely to cover most remittance flows.

6.13. Compiling bilateral remittances data may often require estimations even if aggregate data are available from direct measurement. This is the

[57]"Major partner countries" refers to neighboring countries with substantial current account flows. Examples include Canada and the United States, the members of the European Union, and the members of the Southern African Customs Union.

Box 6.2. Disseminating Bilateral Data: Data from the Deutsche Bundesbank

An example for a regular dissemination of bilateral remittances data is the annual *Special Statistical Publication, Balance of Payments by Region*, published by the Deutsche Bundesbank. This publication is designed to provide more detailed balance of payments data by important partner countries, regions (Africa, Asia, and so forth), and country groups (industrialized countries, developing countries) for all standard items. It is structured according to the balance of payments accounts. It also contains metadata, including general methodological information, data sources, and revision policy. The tables regarding current transfers contain information on public and private transfers with further subdivisions, including data on workers' remittances. Transactions with 20 countries, 5 regions, and 7 country groups for the past four years are shown.

The country breakdown presented in such general publications cannot focus on the country pairs that are most important in the context of remittances. The reason is that in Germany, as in many other countries, transactions such as trade in goods and financial investment are more important for the overall results. The important partner countries are not the same as in the case of remittances. However, such publications can be used as a platform to alert users that detailed data on remittances are available and can be received upon request.

case because data obtained from an ITRS or direct reporting by MTOs may often not identify the partner country correctly, but instead show flows with an international settlement center. It is important that compilers adjust these data adequately, such as by basing their estimations of bilateral flows partly on demographic indicators.

D. Disseminating to Special User Groups

6.14. The users of data on remittances include many groups who are not regular users of other balance of payments data. For example, policymakers, analysts, and activists working on migration require better data on remittances. Providing easier access to relevant data from the balance of payments framework to such groups of users is the motivation for the new data definitions, especially the supplementary items (see Chapter 3).

6.15. The dissemination strategy should account for these data users. They are unlikely to be regular recipients of data through standard dissemination channels for balance of payments statistics. Data users with specific interest in remittances statistics can more easily be reached through focused newsletters, press releases, or special sections on a compiler's website dedicated to remittances data.

6.16. These special data release formats should include both data and metadata. With regard to metadata, it will be important to explain the definitions, statistical techniques, and data limitations in a manner that is accessible to nonspecialists. Data should also be set in context with the country-specific factors that shape them, such as established migration and remittance patterns.

E. Data and Metadata from Experimental Compilation

6.17. Compilation practices for data on remittances are generally less settled than are those on other items in the balance of payments standard presentation. Many countries now review their remittances data, and some are experimenting with new compilation approaches. The data produced by experimental new approaches often differ from those obtained through established methods,

Box 6.3. What Users Need: Tools for Critical Data Use

Compilers should not only practice transparency in data dissemination, but also provide data users with the necessary tools that allow them to access, assess, and use data in an effective manner.

Compilers should provide, and data users should insist on, adequate and current metadata on all data series. Metadata allow users to assess the inherent strengths and weaknesses of data in terms of coverage, valuation, and accuracy. Metadata should include information on data sources, data processing, estimation methods, underlying assumptions, and possible weaknesses of output data, including omissions and divergence in definition.

Compilers should identify, and data users should seek out, official data and distinguish them from other related data series. Nonofficial estimates and forecasts may have useful purposes, but they should not be confused with or misrepresented as official data.

sometimes showing strong fluctuations that cannot be tested for plausibility. In these instances, many compiling agencies are reluctant to release these data.

6.18. However, experimental compilation is an essential step in improving remittances data not only on a country level, but internationally. All compilers of balance of payments data will benefit if compilation experiments and their results are publicly available. It is not suggested that data obtained from experimental compilation exercises be included in the standard balance of payments presentation, unless there are no alternative data. But the data, metadata, and other relevant details of experimental compilation could be published as case studies or working papers. Compilers who do not have adequate publication media may post accounts of their work through interested international organizations or research organizations.

6.19. In some countries, remittances are very important to the overall macroeconomic balance. In this situation, the publication of different or strongly fluctuating estimates should be handled with great care. However, compilers can exchange the results of their experiments with other compilers and legitimate stakeholders. There is little risk in publishing metadata or working papers more widely. Judgment should be used to ensure that the public is informed, not confused, by the discussion of numerous compilation strategies and data sets.

6.20. Compilers should also ensure that data users can clearly distinguish official data—that is, the balance of payments statistics—from other data on remittances that are frequently circulated. When unofficial data are quoted in the media in a misleading manner, compilers should consider an official response. However, official data are not perfect and there are legitimate efforts to improve official estimates. Official data in some instances lack specific detail or coverage that many data users require, and organizations other than official compilers try to meet those needs by manipulating official data. Such data should not be published or be reproduced in a manner that could lead it to be mistaken for official data. Adequate metadata must be provided so that data users can understand how these data are compiled and why these data differ from official estimates (see also Box 6.3).

APPENDIX

I Glossary of Terms

Term	Definition	Source
access point	Location where end users can send or receive remittance transfers. An access point can be physical (e.g., bank branch, post office, shop) or virtual (e.g., website, telephone).	CPSS
account-to-account transfers	Remittance products that require both the sender and the recipient to use a bank account.	OCC
automated clearing house	An electronic clearing system in which payment orders are exchanged among financial institutions, primarily via magnetic media or telecommunications networks, and handled by a data-processing center.	BIS
automated teller machine (ATM)/cash dispenser	An electromechanical device that permits authorized users, typically using machine-readable plastic cards, to withdraw cash from their accounts and access other services, such as balance inquiries, transfer of funds, or acceptance of deposits.	BIS
balance of payments	A system of accounts in which a country records its international transactions. Balance of payments statistics consist of the current account, and the capital and financial account.	IMF
border worker	A worker who regularly (each day or week) crosses a frontier to work in a neighboring country. The border worker is classified as a nonresident of the host country in the balance of payments.	IMF
BPM5	IMF *Balance of Payments Manual*, fifth edition, 1993.	IMF
BPM6	IMF *Balance of Payments and International Investment Position Manual*, sixth edition, 2008.	IMF
capital account	A record of international transactions that includes capital transfers and the acquisition and disposal of nonproduced, nonfinancial assets.	IMF
card-based products	Electronic money products that provide the customer with a portable, specialized computer device, typically an integrated circuit card containing a microprocessor chip.	BIS
cash card	Card for use in only ATMs or cash dispensers.	BIS
cash dispenser	Electromechanical device that permits consumers, typically using machine-readable plastic cards, to withdraw banknotes (currency) and, in some cases, coins. See also "automated teller machine."	BIS
cash remittances	Transfers in the form of money or its equivalent, as opposed to transfers in kind. Physical currency carried from one country to another, to be delivered by or on behalf of the sender to an individual or a family in the receiving country (CEMLA, 2006).	CEMLA
channels of remittances	Different means of sending remittances, such as through banks, money transfer operators, credit unions, and hawala, or by placing a check in the mail, sending funds in the hands of a friend or relative, or carrying the funds oneself to the recipient.	CEMLA
clearing/clearance	The process of transmitting, reconciling, and, in some cases, confirming payment orders or security transfer instructions prior to settlement, including the netting of obligations and the establishment of final positions for settlement. Sometimes the term is used (imprecisely) to include settlement.	BIS
compensation of employees	Wages, salaries, and other compensation in cash or in kind earned by nonresidents for work performed for residents, or earned by residents for work performed for nonresident employers. Nonresident workers are defined as individuals who have been in, and intend to remain in, the host country for less than one year. See also "net compensation of employees" (*BPM6*).	IMF

Note: The Glossary is based on the Glossary of Terms presented in CEMLA (2006).

Term	Definition	Source
correspondent banking	An arrangement under which one bank (correspondent) holds deposits owned by other banks (respondents) and provides payment and other services to those respondent banks. (Cross-border payments are normally made through correspondent banking but may also occur through connected payments systems or connections between central banks.)	CPSS
corridors of remittances	The paths between a specific pair of countries or a specific pair of cities between which international remittances flow.	CEMLA
counterpart data	Statistics from pairs of countries that are linked by the sending and receiving of remittances. Sending country's debits to a receiving country should be comparable with the receiving country's credits from the sending country.	IMF
credit card	A card indicating the holder has been granted a line of credit, enabling the holder to make purchases or withdraw cash up to a prearranged ceiling.	BIS
cross-border netting scheme	An arrangement to net positions or obligations between or among parties in more than one country or jurisdiction.	BIS
cross-border settlement	A settlement that takes place in a country other than the country in which one trade counterparty or both are located.	BIS
current account	In the balance of payments, a record of international transactions that includes trade in goods and services, primary income, and secondary income.	IMF
debit card	Card enabling holders to have their purchases directly charged to funds on their account at a deposit-taking institution (may sometimes be combined with another function, such as that of a cash card or check guarantee card).	BIS
direct participant	A participant in an interbank funds transfer system who is responsible to the settlement agent (or to all other direct participants) for the settlement of its own payments, those of its customers, and those of the indirect participants on whose behalf it is settling.	BIS
draft	A written order from one party (the drawer) to another (the drawee) to pay a specific sum to a party identified on the order (payee) or to the bearer, either on demand (sight draft) or on a specified date (time draft).	BIS
entrepreneurial income	Earnings from self-employment.	IMF
exchange rate differential	Margin by which the foreign exchange rate employed in the transaction exceeds the current interbank or market rate.	CPSS
financial account	In the balance of payments, a record of transactions in financial assets and liabilities that take place between residents and nonresidents.	IMF
financial institution	A category of entities engaged in financial services, including banks, credit unions, savings and loan associations, money transfer operators, microfinance institutions, and currency exchange offices.	FinCEN, Banco de México
forced remittances	An expression referring to the deduction of a portion of migrants' and short-term workers' pay by the governments of sending or receiving countries, or by banks in the migrants' and short-term workers' country of origin, or by employers of migrants and short-term workers, with the intention of ensuring the return of the migrants and short-term workers to their home country or the promotion of investment in that country.	*GEP*
foreign direct investment	The category of international investment associated with a resident entity in one economy (the direct investor) having control or significant influence on the management of an enterprise resident in another economy.	IMF
foreign exchange earnings	Income denominated in a currency other than its own that a country derives from transactions with other countries.	*GEP*
funds transfer system (FTS)	A formal arrangement, based on private contract or statute law, with multiple membership, common rules, and standardized arrangements, for the transmission and settlement of money obligations arising between the members.	BIS
General Data Dissemination System (GDDS)	A set of principles intended to provide guidance for the overall development of macroeconomic, financial, and socio-demographic data with emphasis on progress toward higher-quality data that are disseminated more frequently and in a more timely fashion.	IMF
giro system	A type of credit transfer system.	BIS
gross settlement system	A transfer system in which the settlement of funds (or securities transfer) instructions occurs individually (on an instruction-by-instruction basis).	BIS
hawala remittances	One type of transfers that take place without the intermediation of a formal financial institution. Hawala transfers rely on trust and personal connections. Settlement may occur through goods markets or financial markets.	CEMLA

Term	Definition	Source
home banking	Banking services that a retail customer of a financial institution can access using a telephone, television set, terminal, or personal computer as a telecommunications link to the institution's computer center.	BIS
home country	The country of origin of the migrant and short-term worker (or any other individual).	EU
hometown associations	Organizations and clubs for social, charitable, educational, and civic purposes formed in a host country by migrants and short-term workers who share a hometown in their country of origin.	EU
host country	The country where the migrants and short-term workers work and live.	EU
household	Individuals or group of individuals residing in the same dwelling; a household is a unit for the population census.	EU
household surveys	One method of obtaining information for the estimation of remittance flows.	WB
indirect participant/member	In a funds transfer system, indirect participants are unable to perform some of the system activities (such as input of transfer orders and settlement) and therefore require the services of direct participants to carry out these activities on their behalf.	BIS
informal channels of remittances	An inexact concept that would include sending remittances by means of hawala-type enterprises, placing a check in the mail, sending funds in the hands of a friend or a relative, or carrying the funds oneself to the recipient.	CEMLA, CPSS
informal remittances	See "informal channels of remittances."	CEMLA
informal sector	The exchange of goods and services not accurately recorded in government figures and accounting. The informal economy, which is generally untaxed, commonly includes goods and services including day care, tutoring, or black market exchanges.	WB
interbank funds transfer system	A funds transfer system in which most (or all) direct participants are financial institutions, particularly banks and other credit institutions.	BIS
international bank account number	A globally recognized code that uniquely identifies an account held at a financial institution.	CPSS
International Household Survey Network	An organization established by the World Bank that supports countries in the generation of reliable and timely data, and the harmonization of existing survey instruments.	WB
international remittance transfer	A cross-border, person-to-person payment of relatively low value.	CPSS
international transactions reporting system (ITRS)	An international transactions reporting system measures individual balance of payments cash transactions that pass through domestic banks and though enterprise accounts with banks abroad, noncash transactions, and positions.	IMF
investment income	In the balance of payments, income flows between residents and nonresidents derived from financial assets; the most common types of investment income are income on equity (dividends and reinvested earnings) and income on debt (interests).	IMF
large-value payments	Payments, generally of very large amounts, that are mainly exchanged between banks or between participants in the financial markets and usually require urgent and timely settlement.	BIS
limited-purpose prepaid card	A prepaid card that can be used for a limited number of well-defined purposes. Its use is often restricted to a number of well-identified points of sale within a well-identified location (e.g., a building, corporation, or university). In the case of single-purpose prepaid cards, the card issuer and the service provider may be identical (e.g., cards used in public telephones). See also "prepaid card."	BIS
memorandum item	An item that the IMF recommends for inclusion in the balance of payments to elucidate certain standard components.	IMF
messaging	The arrangements that allow information about a remittance to be passed from the capturing agent to the disbursing agent.	CPSS
metadata	In terms of the balance of payments, metadata consist of descriptions of methodologies, compilation practices, and data sources used by individual countries in compiling their balance of payments accounts.	IMF
migrants' transfers	In the capital account of the balance of payments in *BPM5*, migrants' transfers are contra-entries to the flow of goods (recorded in the current account) and changes in financial items (recorded in the financial account) that arise from the migration (change of residence for at least one year) of individuals from one economy to another. The concept is no longer used in *BPM6*.	IMF

Term	Definition	Source
money order	An instrument used to remit money to the named payee, often used by persons who do not have a checking account relationship with a financial institution, to pay bills or to transfer money to another person or to a company. There are three parties to a money order: the remitter (payer), the payee, and the drawee. Drawees are usually financial institutions or post offices. Payees can either cash their money orders or present them to their bank for collection.	BIS
money transfer company/ money transfer operator (MTO)	Nonbank organizations that are in the business of international remittance transfers.	CEMLA
multifunctional cards	A card that, in addition to a stored value card function, may include other payment facilities, such as a debit or credit card function or nonpayment facilities.	BIS
multilateral netting	An arrangement among three or more parties to net their obligations. The obligations covered by the arrangement may arise from financial contracts, transfers, or both. The multilateral netting of payment obligations normally takes place in the context of a multilateral net settlement system.	BIS
net compensation of employees	Wages, salaries, and other compensation in cash or in kind earned by nonresidents for work performed for a resident less (net of) social contributions, taxes on income, and travel and transportation related to short-term employment. Net compensation of employees is a component of "personal remittances," a supplementary item in the balance of payments.	IMF
net settlement	The settlement of a number of obligations or transfers between or among counterparties on a net basis.	BIS
nonbank financial institution	A financial institution that is not defined as a "bank" (e.g., a financial institution other than a credit institution in Europe or a depository institution in the United States).	BIS
nonprofit institutions serving households (NPISHs)	Nonprofit institutions serving households include hometown associations, charities, churches, disaster relief organizations, and some microfinance organizations that are organized as not-for-profits. In *BPM6*, transfers from NPISHs to households and NPISHs are included in total remittances and transfers to NPISHs.	OECD, SNA
nonresident worker	A person who is employed in an economy other than his or her own economy of residence, including employees of international organizations. A nonresident worker is considered as a "visitor" to the host economy.	IMF
official development aid	Assistance, in cash or in kind, extended to other countries by a government or by an international financial institution.	WB
originator	The purchaser of a remittance product; the initiator of a transfer.	WB, IADB
participant/member	A party who participates in a transfer system. This generic term refers to an institution that is identified by a transfer system (e.g., by a bank identification number) and is allowed to send payment orders directly to the system or that is directly bound by the rules governing the transfer system. See also "indirect participant/member."	BIS
payer	The disbursing agent (entity) in the destination country that pays the recipient of the remittance.	CPSS
payment	The payer's transfer of a monetary claim on a party acceptable to the payee. Typically, claims take the form of banknotes or deposit balances held at a financial institution or at a central bank.	BIS
payment card company	A company that owns trademarks of payment cards (credit, debit, or prepaid cards) and may also provide a number of marketing, processing, or other services to institutions issuing its cards.	BIS
payment instrument	Any instrument enabling the holder/user to transfer funds.	BIS
payment message/ order/ instruction	An order or message to transfer funds (in the form of a monetary claim on a party) to the order of the beneficiary. The order may relate either to a credit transfer or to a debit transfer.	BIS
payment netting	Settling payments due on the same date and in the same currency on a net basis.	BIS
payment system	A payment system consists of a set of instruments, banking procedures, and, typically, interbank funds transfer systems that ensure the circulation of money.	BIS
personal remittances	Personal remittances are personal transfers plus net compensation of employees plus capital transfers between households. This is a supplementary item in the balance of payments.	IMF
personal transfers	Personal transfers consist of all current transfers in cash or in kind made by or received by resident households to or from nonresident households. Personal transfers thus include all current transfers between resident and nonresident individuals. This is a standard item in the balance of payments.	IMF

Term	Definition	Source
point of sale	This term refers to the use of payment cards at a retail location (point of sale). The payment information is captured either by paper vouchers or by electronic terminals, which in some cases are designed also to transmit the information. Where this is so, the arrangement may be referred to as "electronic funds transfer at the point of sale," or EFTPOS.	BIS
prepaid card	A card on which value is stored, and for which the holder has paid the issuer in advance. See "stored value card."	BIS
price (of remittance)	The total cost to the end users of remittance transfers, including fees charged to the sender and the recipient, and the exchange rate differential.	CPSS, WB
public disclosure	Making information publicly accessible, such as by posting on a website or by making copies publicly available.	BIS
real-time transmission, processing, or settlement	The transmission, processing, or settlement of a funds or securities transfer instruction on an individual basis at the time it is initiated.	BIS
remittance service provider/ payment service provider	An entity that provides payment services such as remittances. This includes both deposit-taking entities and non-deposit-takers, such as money transfer operators.	CPSS, WB
remittances	As used in everyday discourse (without regard to formal balance of payments terminology), "remittances" are cross-border payments of relatively low value, often recurrent person-to-person payments by migrants.	CPSS, WB
remittances in kind	Transfers in the form of goods and services as opposed to transfers (remittances) in cash. (See "cash remittances.")	IMF
residence	In the balance of payments, the concept of residence is based on the predominant center of economic interest of an individual or other institutional unit, such as a household, an enterprise, or a nonprofit institution.	IMF
resident	A person is resident in the country where he or she has the predominant center of economic interest. In practice, a person is considered resident in a country if he or she intends to stay in that country for a period of 12 months or longer.	IMF
retail payments	This term describes all payments that are not included in the definition of large-value payments. Retail payments are mainly consumer payments of relatively low value and urgency.	BIS
seasonal worker	One who may, because of seasonal demand for labor, work part of the year in another country and then return to the household in his or her country of residence. Seasonal workers are classified as nonresidents of the host country.	IMF
settlement	An act that discharges obligations with respect to funds (or securities) transfers between two or more parties. See also "gross settlement system" and "net settlement."	BIS
smart card	An integrated circuit card with a microprocessor, capable of performing calculations.	BIS
social benefits	Current transfers (including pensions), received by households from corporations, government, and nonprofit institutions, and intended to provide for sickness, unemployment, retirement, housing, education, and other circumstances.	IMF, SNA
social contributions	Actual or imputed payments to social insurance schemes to make provision for social insurance benefits to be paid.	IMF, SNA
stored value card	A prepaid card on which the record of funds can be increased as well as decreased.	BIS
supplementary item	An item that should be considered for inclusion in the balance of payments when a country believes such information would be of interest to analysts and policymakers.	IMF
SWIFT	Society for Worldwide Interbank Financial Telecommunication (SWIFT): a cooperative organization created and owned by banks that operates a network that facilitates the exchange of payment and other financial messages between financial institutions (including broker-dealers and securities companies) throughout the world. A SWIFT payment message is an instruction to transfer funds; the exchange of funds (settlement) subsequently takes place over a payment system or through correspondent banking relationships.	BIS
System of National Accounts	A comprehensive set of macroeconomic accounts created jointly by the International Monetary Fund, the European Union, the Organization for Economic Cooperation and Development, the United Nations, and the World Bank.	SNA
threshold of reporting	The value above which a transaction must by law be reported to government authorities.	IMF
total remittances	The sum of personal remittances and social benefits. Social benefits include benefits payable under social security funds and pension funds. Total remittances will be recorded as a supplementary item in the balance of payments.	IMF
total remittances and transfers to NPISHs	Total remittances plus current and capital transfers to NPISHs. This is a supplementary item in the balance of payments.	IMF

Term	Definition	Source
transfers	Offset entries in the balance of payments to the provision of economic values provided and received without a quid pro quo, such as grants and gifts in cash or in kind. "Current transfers" affect the level of income and consumption of goods and services. "Capital transfers" result in a commensurate change in the stocks of assets of one or both parties to the transaction.	IMF
unbanked	Segments of the population who do not have access to a bank account and other banking services, or who choose not to avail themselves of such services. (The "unbanked" may include senders and recipients of remittances.)	
user	Payment system users comprise both participants and their customers for payment services.	BIS
workers' remittances	In *BPM5*, workers' remittances comprise current transfers by migrants who are employed in their host countries and considered residents there (i.e., who have stayed or are expected to stay for one year or longer).	IMF

Note on abbreviations used in sources: Where a term or a definition is taken or adapted from a particular source, the source is indicated in abbreviated form. Terms for which no source is given originated in academic institutions or in the remittance market. The abbreviations are explained in the List of Abbreviations.

APPENDIX

2 Data Quality Assessment Framework: Generic Framework

Quality Dimensions	Elements	Indicators
0. Prerequisites of quality	**0.1 Legal and institutional environment**—*The environment is supportive of statistics.*	0.1.1 The responsibility for collecting, processing, and disseminating the statistics is clearly specified. 0.1.2 Data sharing and coordination among data-producing agencies are adequate. 0.1.3 Individual reporters' data are to be kept confidential and used for statistical purposes only. 0.1.4 Statistical reporting is ensured through legal mandate and/or measures to encourage response.
	0.2 Resources—*Resources are commensurate with needs of statistical programs.*	0.2.1 Staff, facilities, computing resources, and financing are commensurate with statistical programs. 0.2.2 Measures to ensure efficient use of resources are implemented.
	0.3 Relevance—*Statistics cover relevant information on the subject field.*	0.3.1 The relevance and practical utility of existing statistics in meeting users' needs are monitored.
	0.4 Other quality management—*Quality is a cornerstone of statistical work.*	0.4.1 Processes are in place to focus on quality. 0.4.2 Processes are in place to monitor the quality of the statistical program. 0.4.3 Processes are in place to deal with quality considerations in planning the statistical program.
1. Assurances of integrity *The principle of objectivity in the collection, processing, and dissemination of statistics is firmly adhered to.*	**1.1 Professionalism**—*Statistical policies and practices are guided by professional principles.*	1.1.1 Statistics are produced on an impartial basis. 1.1.2 Choices of sources and statistical techniques as well as decisions about dissemination are informed solely by statistical considerations. 1.1.3 The appropriate statistical entity is entitled to comment on erroneous interpretation and misuse of statistics.
	1.2 Transparency—*Statistical policies and practices are transparent.*	1.2.1 The terms and conditions under which statistics are collected, processed, and disseminated are available to the public. 1.2.2 Internal governmental access to statistics prior to their release is publicly identified. 1.2.3 Products of statistical agencies/units are clearly identified as such. 1.2.4 Advance notice is given of major changes in methodology, source data, and statistical techniques.
	1.3 Ethical standards—*Policies and practices are guided by ethical standards.*	1.3.1 Guidelines for staff behavior are in place and are well known to the staff.
2. Methodological soundness *The methodological basis for the statistics follows internationally accepted standards, guidelines, or good practices.*	**2.1 Concepts and definitions**—*Concepts and definitions used are in accord with internationally accepted statistical frameworks.*	2.1.1 The overall structure in terms of concepts and definitions follows internationally accepted standards, guidelines, or good practices.
	2.2 Scope—*The scope is in accord with internationally accepted standards, guidelines, or good practices.*	2.2.1 The scope is broadly consistent with internationally accepted standards, guidelines, or good practices.
	2.3 Classification/ sectorization—*Classification and sectorization systems are in accord with internationally accepted standards, guidelines, or good practices.*	2.3.1 Classification/sectorization systems used are broadly consistent with internationally accepted standards, guidelines, or good practices.
	2.4 Basis for recording—*Flows and stocks are valued and recorded according to internationally accepted standards, guidelines, or good practices.*	2.4.1 Market prices are used to value flows and stocks. 2.4.2 Recording is done on an accrual basis. 2.4.3 Grossing/netting procedures are broadly consistent with internationally accepted standards, guidelines, or good practices.

Quality Dimensions	Elements	Indicators
3. Accuracy and reliability *Source data and statistical techniques are sound and statistical outputs sufficiently portray reality.*	**3.1 Source data**—*Source data available provide an adequate basis to compile statistics.*	3.1.1 Source data are obtained from comprehensive data collection programs that take into account country-specific conditions. 3.1.2 Source data reasonably approximate the definitions, scope, classifications, valuation, and time of recording required. 3.1.3 Source data are timely.
	3.2 Assessment of source data—*Source data are regularly assessed.*	3.2.1 Source data—including censuses, sample surveys, and administrative records—are routinely assessed, e.g., for coverage, sample error, response error, and non-sampling error; the results of the assessments are monitored and made available to guide statistical processes.
	3.3 Statistical techniques—*Statistical techniques employed conform to sound statistical procedures.*	3.3.1 Data compilation employs sound statistical techniques to deal with data sources. 3.3.2 Other statistical procedures (e.g., data adjustments and transformations, and statistical analysis) employ sound statistical techniques.
	3.4 Assessment and validation of intermediate data and statistical outputs—*Intermediate results and statistical outputs are regularly assessed and validated.*	3.4.1 Intermediate results are validated against other information where applicable. 3.4.2 Statistical discrepancies in intermediate data are assessed and investigated. 3.4.3 Statistical discrepancies and other potential indicators or problems in statistical outputs are investigated.
	3.5 Revision studies—*Revisions, as a gauge of reliability, are tracked and mined for the information they may provide.*	3.5.1 Studies and analyses of revisions are carried out routinely and used internally to inform statistical processes (see also 4.3.3).
4. Serviceability *Statistics, with adequate periodicity and timeliness, are consistent and follow a predictable revision policy.*	**4.1 Periodicity and timeliness**—*Periodicity and timeliness follow internationally accepted dissemination standards.*	4.1.1 Periodicity follows dissemination standards. 4.1.2 Timeliness follows dissemination standards.
	4.2 Consistency—*Statistics are consistent within the data set, over time, and with major data sets.*	4.2.1 Statistics are consistent within the data set. 4.2.2 Statistics are consistent or reconcilable over a reasonable period of time. 4.2.3 Statistics are consistent or reconcilable with those obtained through other data sources and/or statistical frameworks.
	4.3 Revision policy and practice—*Data revisions follow a regular and publicized procedure.*	4.3.1 Revisions follow a regular and transparent schedule. 4.3.2 Preliminary and/or revised data are clearly identified. 4.3.3 Studies and analyses of revisions are made public (see also 3.5.1).
5. Accessibility *Data and metadata are easily available, and assistance to users is adequate.*	**5.1 Data accessibility**—*Statistics are presented in a clear and understandable manner, forms of dissemination are adequate, and statistics are made available on an impartial basis.*	5.1.1 Statistics are presented in a way that facilitates proper interpretation and meaningful comparisons (layout and clarity of text, tables, and charts). 5.1.2 Dissemination media and format are adequate. 5.1.3 Statistics are released on a preannounced schedule. 5.1.4 Statistics are made available to all users at the same time. 5.1.5 Statistics not routinely disseminated are made available upon request.
	5.2 Metadata accessibility—*Up-to-date and pertinent metadata are made available.*	5.2.1 Documentation on concepts, scope, classifications, basis of recording, data sources, and statistical techniques is available, and differences from internationally accepted standards, guidelines, or good practices are annotated. 5.2.2 Levels of detail are adapted to the needs of the intended audience.
	5.3 Assistance to users—*Prompt and knowledgeable support service is available.*	5.3.1 Contact points for each subject field are publicized. 5.3.2 Catalogs of publications, documents, and other services, including information on any charges, are widely available.

Bibliography

Bank of Spain, 2006, "Workers' Remittances in the Spanish Balance of Payments," *Economic Bulletin* (July). Available via the Internet: www.bde.es/informes/be/boleco/2006/be0607e.pdf.

Bilsborrow, R.E., Graeme Hugo, A.S. Oberai, and Hania Zlotnik, 1997, *International Migration Statistics: Guidelines for Improving Data Collection Systems* (Geneva: International Labour Office).

Bouhga-Hagbe, Jacques, 2004, "A Theory of Workers' Remittances with an Application to Morocco," IMF Working Paper 04/194 (Washington: International Monetary Fund).

Centre for Latin American Monetary Studies (CEMLA), 2006, *Draft Manual on Best Practices for the Compilation of International Remittances* (Mexico City). Available via the Internet: www.cemla-remesas.org/PDF/MBP.pdf.

Committee on Payment and Settlement Systems (CPSS), 2004, "Survey of Developments in Electronic Money and Internet and Mobile Payments," CPSS Publication No. 62 (Basel, Switzerland: Bank for International Settlements, March).

———, and World Bank, 2006, "General Principles for International Remittance Services," Consultative Report, CPSS Publication No. 73 (Basel, Switzerland: Bank for International Settlements and World Bank, March).

de Luna Martinez, Jose, 2005, "Workers' Remittances to Developing Countries: A Survey with Central Banks on Selected Public Policy Issues," Policy Research Working Paper No. 3638 (Washington: World Bank).

El Qorchi, Mohammed, Samuel Munzele Maimbo, and John F. Wilson, 2003, *Informal Funds Transfer Systems: An analysis of the informal Hawala System*, IMF Occasional Paper No. 222 (Washington: International Monetary Fund).

Eurostat, Committee on Monetary, Financial and Balance of Payments Statistics, 2003, *Final Report of the Technical Group on Direct Reporting* (Luxembourg, September).

Faini, Riccardo, 1994, "Workers Remittances and Real Exchange Rate: A Quantitative Framework," *Journal of Population Economics*, Vol. 7, No. 2, pp. 235–45.

International Monetary Fund, 1993, *Balance of Payments Manual* (Washington, 5th ed.).

———, 2007, *Balance of Payments Statistics Yearbook*, Parts 2 and 3 (Washington).

———, 2008, *Balance of Payments and International Investment Position Manual* (Washington, 6th ed.).

Kish, Leslie, 1965, *Survey Sampling* (New York: John Wiley & Sons).

Maphosa, France, 2005, "The Impact of Remittances from Zimbabweans Working in South Africa on Rural Livelihoods in the Southern Districts of Zimbabwe," Forced Migration Working Paper Series No. 14 (Witwatersrand, South Africa: University of Witwatersrand).

McKenzie, David, and Johan Mistiaen, 2007, "Surveying Migrant Households: A Comparison of Census-based, Snowball, and Intercept Point Surveys," Policy Research Working Paper No. 4419 (Washington: World Bank).

Orozco, Manuel, 2004, *The Remittance Marketplace: Prices, Policy and Financial Institutions* (Washington: Institute for the Study of International Migration, Georgetown University, June).

Schiopu, Ioana, and Nikolaus Siegfried, 2006, *Determinants of Workers' Remittances—Evidence from the European Neighbouring Region*, ECB Working Paper No. 688 (Brussels: European Central Bank).

U.K. Remittance Working Group, 2005, *U.K. Remittance Market* (London: Profile Business Intelligence Ltd.).

United Nations, 2005a, *Designing Household Survey Samples: Practical Guidelines*, Studies in Methods, Series F No. 98 (New York: Department of Economic and Social Affairs, Statistics Division).

———, 2005b, *Household Sample Surveys in Developing and Transition Countries,* Studies and Methods, Series F No. 96 (New York: Department of Economic and Social Affairs, Statistics Division).

World Bank, 2008a, *Migration and Remittances Factbook* (Washington).

———, 2008b, *World Development Indicators* (Washington).

Index